BERLITZ

AMSTERDAM

- A ✅ in the text denotes a highly recommended sight
- A complete A–Z of practical information starts on p. 111
- Extensive mapping throughout: on cover flaps and in text

Printed in Switzerland by Weber SA, Bienne.

2nd edition (1995/1996)

Although we make every effort to ensure the accuracy of the information in this guide, changes do occur. If you have any new information, suggestions or corrections to contribute, we would like to hear from you. Please write to Berlitz Publishing at the above address.

Text:	Martin Gostelow
Editor:	Sarah Hudson
Photography:	Jon Davison
Cartography:	Falk-Verlag, Hamburg
Layout:	Icon Associates, Chesham

Thanks to the Amsterdam Tourist Office (VVV), Tonie van Marle and Sealink Stena Line for their valuable assistance in the preparation of this guide.

CONTENTS

Amsterdam and its People

There's nowhere quite like Amsterdam, one of Europe's architectural jewels. Although not the seat of government of The Netherlands (that's 40 minutes down the road in The Hague, where the queen also resides), it's the undisputed capital of trade, finance and culture. A blend of good cheer and hard-headed business sense, it quickly feels like home to visitors, once they begin to understand the different facets of the city. Those can be as varied as the personalities depicted by the Old Masters in their paintings – firmly upright citizens one minute, revellers in anarchic tavern scenes the next.

Arrive on a Sunday morning and you'll think a pied piper has led the entire population away and left a ghost city, quiet and reverential.

All the working week the denizens are back with a vengeance, busily trying to make money, unloading giant trucks in impossible alleys, and blocking lesser vehicles with complete disdain. You'll have to dodge the hordes of cyclists, who apparently believe themselves immune from danger as they whip and weave through the congestion. Comes a lull in the traffic. The bells of the Westerkerk break through from Amsterdam's tallest church tower, playing 'John Brown's Body' or some other unlikely tune. The Mint Tower carillon chimes in, and so do the bells of the old Royal (Koninklijk) Palace on Dam Square. Below, amid the shopping crowds, one of the city's street organs grinds away.

Blunder into Europe's most outrageous red-light district on a Saturday night and you might think you've been transported to one of Bangkok's sleazier districts. In spite of the explicit window displays, it's all seen as rather a joke by the curious crowds, who wander up and down with no apparent intention of patronizing the facilities. They can hardly be good for trade, as **5**

Traditional Dutch dress is often kept for special occasions nowadays.

anyone who was thinking of participating might be deterred by such an audience. Then it's Sunday again and Amsterdam assumes its face of innocence, the perfect picture postcard.

The heart of the city is a miracle of survival, a unique museum of 17th-century architecture and urban planning. **6** Can there ever have been a more compatible marriage of function and form, designed here to match the needs of a great trading port? Houses and warehouses face canals linked like veins and arteries to the docks where huge three-masters of the Dutch East Indies Company once unloaded the world's most desirable commodities. The Venice of the North, it has often been called. Row after row of old gabled houses lean crazily against one another along the tree-fringed waterways, where houseboats line up like parked cars.

If this is a museum, it's a lived-in one. Instead of emptying out at six o'clock in the evening, the commuting pattern typical of other cities is reversed. The trucks disappear, but many workers will stream out of modern offices and factories in the suburbs and return to their homes in the centre. They'll be back amid their local shops, in village-like streets between the canals, where there's still a friendly baker and grocer and an open-air market just a short walk away. Equally important, one of Amsterdam's brown cafés, wood-panelled and nicotine-stained, will be just round the corner. Any spot of sun or a warm evening brings people pouring out onto the canal banks and filling all the chairs in the open-air cafés.

The local partiality for the traditional life is largely shared by the city authorities.

The picturesque Golden Age character of the central area is preserved by statute. Thousands of warehouses and houses are classified as protected monuments. But there hasn't always been such agreement: the 1960s and 70s were marked by violent rows whenever any building was threatened, whether it was for

Countless lights decorate bridges along the main waterways, creating a magical, fairytale picture at night.

offices, public housing or for the construction of the metro. Supported by countless millions of wooden piles, the old city was built on land won by sheer hard work and a genius for hydraulic engineering. Today's Amsterdammers are not going to let their precious inheritance be jeopardized by philistine developers. Seventeenth century residential areas are renovated in their entirety, and if gaps are filled by an office building, it has to be in sympathetic style. New hotels, offices, low-cost housing and luxury apartments have nevertheless appeared, but they are outside the old centre, along the dockside waterfront and the riverbanks.

Strand three Amsterdammers on a desert island, it's said, and they'll organise three political parties. They love a friendly argument, particularly if they can shock the

rest of conformist Holland. They have loud discussions in bars. They parade with banners the way other people change their socks. Underdogs are sure of support in this city. Intolerance is condemned (admittedly with a degree of vigour approaching intolerance itself). Even a City Hall booklet admits with a sort of perverse pride that of 700,000 Amsterdammers, 699,999 are obstinate Amsterdammers.

But Amsterdam has always been an innovator too, claiming to have introduced the first postal service, the first municipal fire brigade, workshops for special needs, braille-marked money and grants for 'living art' (given to street entertainers).

Along with London, Paris and Rome, Amsterdam is one of Europe's most popular tourist cities. This is in part due to the great art galleries,

*A*ny warm evening will tempt Amsterdammers out to the canal banks and cafés.

the fascinating architecture, and the chance to take excursions to the villages and springtime tulip fields, and in part attributable to the warm-hearted welcome the people extend to visitors. Ask them the way, and there's not a gram of resentment if you don't speak difficult Dutch. They will answer you in English, German or French, perhaps Spanish and Italian, too, and if you come up with a language that beats them they'll ask the next passer-by for help.

If you are willing to experiment a little, eating out can be an adventure, with anything from traditional raw herring to an Indonesian *rijsttafel* on the menu. Other many and varied cuisines range from Italian to Thai, Argentine to Turkish. As likely as not, they'll be prepared by the people who know them best. More than a hundred different nationalities live side by side in the city, on the whole harmoniously. After 300 years of religious and political tolerance the predominant attitude is one of live and let live, **9**

Traditional gabled warehouses can be strikingly adapted for new uses.

albeit often in mutual incomprehension.

Not only are houses preserved here, but social habits as well: it's like a time capsule of attitudes and modes of dress. Ever since the student revolutions of the 1960s, the youth of Europe and the rest of the world still see Amsterdam as the venue of a continuous free party. They may be disappointed: life is tougher these days and the face of the city is not without its blemishes. Graffiti are everywhere, and unemployment is worryingly higher than the national aver-

age, especially among the more recent immigrants. Amsterdam's present economy requires people with education and training and there's not much that those without these can legally do.

Other once notorious problems seem nowadays to be less visible. The housing shortage that once plagued the city, and which created an army of squatters, has abated. And the drug epidemic, with its attendant violence, appears to be somewhat stabilized. Indeed, the authorities claim that hard drug use is in decline and street crime is being reduced, with the aid of a police flying squad on mountain bikes.

In short, the city is facing the kind of difficulties familiar to most of the world's large cities and is trying, as always, to find reasonable and equitable solutions.

A Brief History

The marshy flood plain of the River Amstel, adjoining the Zuider Zee, was an unpromising site. For one thing, the land was frequently flooded during North Sea storms. According to evocative legend, the first settlers were Batavians who had floated down the Rhine in hollowed-out tree trunks. Somehow, they managed to create enough dry ground to live on. Thus began a tradition of channelling and managing rivers and the sea that was to be carried on by their successors right up to modern times.

The Romans, who came here in order to trade more than to conquer, record the presence in this area of the Batavians and related tribes, including the Frisians, shortly before the birth of Christ. Afterwards, the Franks, Saxons and others expanded into the area during the massive migrations of the Germanic peoples in the 5th century which heralded the beginning of the Dark Ages.

Christianity, which had established a tenuous hold under Roman influence, was vanquished, and, despite the efforts of a handful of courageous missionaries, more than 300 years passed before the pagan tribes were converted.

Not until well into the Middle Ages did the descendants of these peoples start to impinge upon the great events which were slowly forging a new Europe after the fall of the Roman empire. Charlemagne and his empire came and went, and The Netherlands remained an amalgam of small states ruled by counts, dukes and bishops.

One group, probably the Waterlanders from the region just north of the IJ (a long broad inlet from the Zuider Zee), moved to slightly less waterlogged ground and beached their boats on a sandbank where the River Amstel runs into the River IJ (IJ is pronounced somewhere between 'eye' and 'ay' and is treated as a single letter in Dutch). They dammed the river to prevent the tides **11** sweeping in. As a consequence of the dam, all cargoes had to be transhipped between sea-going and river vessels, providing a further lucrative source of revenue for the community.

The settlement took the name of Amstelredamme. The dam was situated exactly where Dam Square and the Koninklijk Paleis (Royal Palace) are today.

In 1275, Count Floris V of Holland granted a toll freedom to the local citizenry, and it is from this year onwards that the people of Amsterdam traditionally count the founding of their city.

From Fishing Village to Trading Port

At first, the expansion of the Waterlanders' settlement was hardly spectacular. But in 1345 an incongruous occurrence provided a turning point for the community's fortunes. A piece of communion bread a sick man had tried unsuccessfully to swallow failed to burn in the fireplace. The event was declared a miracle, and as a result, Amsterdam became a place of pilgrimage for Christians of the Middle Ages.

Thereafter, commerce thrived. More and more ships used the port, sailing in from the Baltic, from France, and from England, past the northern island of Texel and down the shallow Zuider Zee to a safe anchorage at sheltered Amsterdam.

In 1452, fire almost destroyed the wooden town, and

*A*msterdam in 1538 shows the heart of today's city (painting by Jan Christiaansen Micker).

from then on it became compulsory to build with bricks. Colourful gables also replaced the old wooden signs denoting trades, professions and names, and the town took on a permanent look. By the beginning of the 16th century, Amsterdam counted 2000 houses and a number of monasteries and convents, with 15,000 inhabitants. During the next 50 years it almost trebled in size. The most significant factor in the rapid 16th-century growth was the general spirit of revolt against Spanish domination of the region. While most of the Low Countries laboured under harsh foreign rule, Amsterdam was neutral for a long time, attracting large numbers of refugees, such as the diamond-cutters from Spanish-devastated Antwerp.

Under Spanish Yoke

After centuries of belonging to nobody but themselves, most of the Low Countries (the present-day Netherlands and Belgium) had, in the early 15th century, fallen under the **13** sway of the Burgundians, a once-powerful state whose Dukes' bequest to posterity has been the name of a celebrated wine-producing region of France. In 1506, as a result of a series of treaties, intrigues deaths and marriages, these territories became part of the inheritance which eventually established Charles, Duke of Burgundy (a Hapsburg) as Holy Roman Emperor and King of Spain, ruler of a realm in which, it was claimed, 'the sun never set'.

Though Charles V was born in Flanders, Spain was the heart of his empire. He proved less than sympathetic to his subjects back in The Netherlands, whose increasing wealth made them a target for heavy imperial taxation. Above all, Charles was fiercely opposed to the challenge put forward by the Reformation to the Catholic church, the papacy and Catholic rulers such as himself.

The Reformation had spread outwards from Germany to become firmly rooted in the northern, Dutch, areas of Spain's Netherlands province, and in an attempt to burn out the infection, Charles introduced the Inquisition in the 1520s.

Charles' successor, his son Philip II of Spain, pursued the anti-Reformation policy with the utmost vigour. In 1567 he sent the ruthless Duke of Alva to The Netherlands to settle the religious issue and establish a military dictatorship.

Struggle for Independence

An era of terror and torture began – a period of warfare which was to last 80 years. Out of the resistance emerged the liberal thinker and spirited leader of the Dutch rebels, Prince William (who was dubbed William the Silent) of the House of Orange, whose forebears originally came from the former minor principality of Orange, just north of Avignon in the Rhône valley. He had, however, inherited extensive estates in The Netherlands, hence his involvement in the struggle, and he was to be the founder of the dynasty which has reigned as *stadhouder* (governor), or monarch, over The Netherlands ever since.

His cause continued to gather momentum, especially after the brutal 1572 massacre of the Protestant Huguenots in France. While violence raged all over the country with many towns – including Alkmaar, Haarlem and Leiden – suffering the hardships of battle, siege or occupation, Amsterdam remained loyal to the King of Spain. It wasn't until 1578 that this trading city, already renowned for its religious tolerance (it had taken in Portuguese Jews fleeing from the Inquisition, Protestant Huguenots persecuted in France and English dissenters), finally declared its desire for freedom from Spanish rule.

In 1579, the seven, largely Protestant, provinces north of the Rhine (known as the United Provinces) concluded the Treaty of Utrecht, and before long this break between the northern and southern provinces became permanent. In the south (where many of the people were French-speaking Walloons), even Catholics had joined in the resistance against the tyranny of the Spaniards. However, the Spanish army had managed to maintain its hold on these areas, and the long-term consequence of the ensuing north-south split was the separate existence of today's Netherlands and Belgium.

Meanwhile, prior to his murder in 1584, William had become the founding father of Dutch independence – at the same time that Elizabeth's England was also defying the Spain of Philip II. The struggle was illustriously pursued by William's sons, Maurice and Frederick Henry.

More territory was subsequently gained in the south and south east of the country, and when the treaties of The Hague and of Westphalia were signed in 1648, the independent state of The Netherlands came into being within boundaries which have scarcely changed since.

15

The Golden Age

Even before The Netherlands gained their freedom from Spain, the Dutch Golden Age had begun to burgeon. In the early 16th century, the Dutch had already provided northern Europe with its greatest representative of the Renaissance – the philosopher Erasmus. The combined skills of the merchant class, scientists, artists, and craftsmen, both native and imported, created a climate so fertile that one enterprise followed another and turned the 17th century into that of Holland's glory.

By the end of the 15th century, the Portuguese had pioneered the sea route to the East, and Lisbon became an emporium for the products of India and the East Indies. Dutch merchants began buying these up and shipping them to northern Europe where they were sold for a considerable profit. It was a natural step (provoked by Spain's conquest of Portugal) to extend their voyages and fetch the merchandise themselves from the Far East. As competition grew and profits fell, Amsterdam's shipowners united to form a single company, known as the Dutch East Indies Company *(Verenigde Oostindische Compagnie, or VOC)*, which was granted a monopoly for trade with all countries east of the Cape of Good Hope. It soon

Fishing boats on the IJsselmeer have scarcely changed in design for 300 years.

became one of the most powerful commercial organizations the world had ever known. At its height, the VOC commanded 150 merchant ships, 40 warships and 10,000 soldiers. Under its flag sailed some of Holland's greatest sea heroes. It paid a dividend of 40 per cent, and Amsterdam was its biggest and most influential shareholder.

The VOC's major foreign base was Batavia (Jakarta) on Java, but from Amsterdam, Henry Hudson was also sent in search of a new route to China. Instead, in 1609, he discovered the river that bears his name and founded the settlement of New Amsterdam, the forerunner of New York City, on the island of Manhattan (until then undiscovered), which was purchased from the local Indians in exchange for cloth and trinkets in 1626.

Dutch sailors of the VOC were the first white men to land in Australia, 150 years before Captain Cook. Abel Tasman charted much of its coastline and discovered Tasmania, New Zealand and the Fiji Islands. In 1652 Jan van Riebeeck created a victualling and medical station at Cape Town, the halfway point along the Dutch route to the East. Ceylon (Sri Lanka) was colonized, as were parts of Brazil and the Caribbean. The Dutch island trading post, situated off Nagasaki, was the only one allowed to deal with Japan during the 200 years of the Shogun isolation.

If Far Eastern trade was more exotic, and extremely profitable, European commerce remained even more important. In a long-established business, casks of salted herring, with the salt brought from Portugal and timber for the barrels from the Baltic, were exported to Russia.

Merchandise from as far a field as the White Sea and the Mediterranean was shipped to Amsterdam by Dutch merchants and sold for lucrative profits throughout western Europe.

Even English and French coastal trade was largely in Dutch hands. **17**

The Fruits of Enterprise

All this brought tremendous wealth to The Netherlands (whose population was little more than one million) and most of all to Amsterdam, which controlled 50 per cent of all Dutch trade.

Amsterdam had become the greatest port and market in the world and, with its inhabitants now numbering 200,000, was bursting at the seams. Its original crescent of canals was extended outwards around the River Amstel, in the horseshoe layout we see today.

As industry and commerce expanded, pinnacles were reached in the arts, particularly painting. This was the age of Rembrandt, Frans Hals, Jan Steen, Vermeer and Paulus Potter, to name but a few.

It was at this time, too, that Dutch scientists and military men gained world respect. Antonie van Leeuwenhoek invented the microscope. Herman Boerhaave's lectures in medicine attracted students from all over Europe. Prince Maurice, son of William the Silent, had developed new, sophisticated military tactics which now spread over the continent.

The rise of the United Provinces to a position of eminence as the world's foremost maritime power led to rivalry with England, which erupted in a series of wars between the two countries. In the second Anglo-Dutch war (1665-67), England was nearly brought to its knees when Holland's greatest sea hero, Admiral de Ruyter, caused great panic in London by his audacious raid up the River Medway as far as Chatham to burn the English fleet and tow home in triumph the flagship *Royal Charles*, part of whose stern decoration can still be seen in the Rijksmuseum.

Decline

Soon the dynamic and profitable energy of the 1600s began to flag; and the 18th century was a quiet period, characterized more by an aping of the French way of life than by anything indigenous.

Holland and The Netherlands

To a Dutchman, the word Holland does not mean the whole country. That's The Netherlands.

North Holland (which includes Amsterdam) and South Holland (including The Hague and Rotterdam) are just two of the country's 12 provinces.

The other 10 are: Drenthe, Friesland, Gelderland, Groningen, Limburg, North Brabant, Overijssel, Utrecht, Flevoland and Zeeland.

In 1776, England's rebellious North American colonies found a ready ally in The Netherlands. Amsterdam merchants supplied them, via the Dutch Caribbean island of St. Eustatius, with much-needed arms and ammunition, and made huge loans to set the new country on its feet.

These actions incurred British wrath, then the Anglo-Dutch war of 1780, during which British sea supremacy sounded the death knell of the once-powerful Dutch trading companies. Prosperity in Amsterdam declined. Finally, in 1795, Napoleon's armies overran the United Provinces and the Golden Age became just a memory.

The years of French rule saw an upturn in elegance and culture for Amsterdam, but was a low point for commercial activity. Louis Bonaparte, younger brother of Napoléon, was installed as King of Holland and turned the town hall on Dam Square into his own private palace - the Koninklijk Paleis (see also p.31). In 1810 he fled the city overnight after severe criticism of his lax administration.

Holland now lost any semblance of independence and was completely annexed by France. In 1813, as the star of Napoléon began to sink, the exiled Prince William of Orange was recalled and proclaimed king.

19

A Modern Nation Develops

With the establishment of this new monarchy, the modern-day Netherlands were born. The 19th century was one of steady progress for Amsterdam. The economic rot had first to be halted – then came the simultaneous problems and advantages of the industrial revolution.

Vast new housing areas were needed, some of which soon degenerated into slums. But as the century advanced, better homes were built, along with museums. The basis of Holland's social welfare system was laid down during this period and, in the diamond industry, workers formed a trade union that was said to be the model of modern day unionism.

Gables and Gablestones

Look up at the gables and *gevelstenen* (gablestones) on the old buildings. These date from before the French occupation of 1795.

Gablestones were a pictorial language of their own. They were sculpted, and often coloured, symbols of an owner's name, town of origin, religious belief or, more usually, his occupation.

An ox-head still adorning Nieuwendijk 406 refers back to a former owner who was a hide dealer. A gablestone showing a man wielding a scythe at Bethaniëndwarsstraat 18 dates back to 1623.

There are also city scenes and lambs, blacksmiths and grain carriers – and a yawning man in Gravenstraat, the traditional sign for a druggist.

This Amsterdam address system baffled the French who promptly numbered the houses in each street.

To revitalize Amsterdam's port, the North Holland Canal was dug from Den Helder in the north, and the even more important North Sea Canal from IJmuiden on the coast.

The 20th Century

After the First World War, during which Holland remained neutral, spectacular progress was made in land reclamation from the sea: in

the 1920s and 30s, the old, tidal Zuider Zee was transformed into a freshwater lake by the construction of the 19-mile enclosing dike *(Afsluitdijk)*, and its waters were partially pumped out to create new land.

During the Second World War, however, Holland was not so lucky. Despite its protestations of neutrality, it was invaded by the Germans in spring 1940. Five years of hardship followed.

Despite a particularly courageous protest strike mounted in 1941 by Dutch dockworkers, most of Amsterdam's Jews were sent to concentration camps. After the Allied advance was halted, the winter of 1944-45 was one of near-starvation in Amsterdam and the north. The valiant will of the Dutch to survive as an independent nation was undoubtedly bolstered by Queen Wilhelmina's defiant broadcasts from London, where she had taken refuge only after extreme diplomatic pressure.

Added to the devastation of the war, The Netherlands also **21** had to face the loss of its colonial possessions in the East Indies, now independent Indonesia. But this generated a will to work for recovery which hallmarked the post-war years. Industry grew, at the same time a highly advanced welfare system was developed and legislation was introduced to protect the architectural character of many of the city's buildings.

The Dutch today are firm supporters of European integration. and the economy of The Netherlands has flourished, with the guilder (or *gulden*) being one of the strongest of the European currencies.

Yet all this security and prosperity hasn't led to complacency. One thing is certain, if you know Amsterdammers: restless merchant-adventurers at heart, they are not a people to stand still for very long.

Springtime in Amsterdam, the best time to visit, dresses trees in bright new growth.

Where to Go

Amsterdam has great advantages for the visitor. It's compact and a real pleasure to walk in. Many places of interest are concentrated in a small area and are easy to reach on foot. The rest can be reached by an excellent public transport system, or a slightly longer walk. Be sure to bring your most comfortable walking shoes to deal with the cobbled streets. Perhaps best of all in good weather is the favourite local means of transport – a bicycle.

It can seem confusing at first: an apparent maze of canals, all roughly the same size, all tree-lined and hemmed in by rows of tightly-packed gabled buildings. The effect is enchanting, but the height of the houses makes it difficult to spot landmarks and get your bearings. Pause and take a good look at our map on the cover flap of this guide.

Central Amsterdam is like a horseshoe of canals split down the middle by the Damrak-Rokin-Vijzelstraat main street. Major canal (*gracht*) names to note are: the **Singel** (meaning ring or girdle and not to be confused with the Singelgracht, another encircling canal further out); the **Herengracht** (Gentlemen's Canal); the **Keizersgracht** (Emperor's Canal); and the **Prinsengracht** (Princes' Canal). Moving out from the centre, the initials 'H-K-P' of these three come conveniently in alphabetical order to help you remember which comes next.

The coloured sections of the map on the cover correspond to the way we have divided the city for sightseeing in the following pages, but before setting out to explore any of the sights, we suggest that you **take to the water.**

The city is divided into four sections. These can be taken in any order, but we have chosen to begin with the area which includes the three great art museums (the Rijksmuseum, the Vincent van Gogh Museum and the Stedelijk Museum), all of which are high on most visitors' list of priorities.

Canal Tours

The best introduction to the city is to take a trip on one of the many tour boats. The main boarding points are: near Centraal Station; Stadhouderskade near Leidseplein; and on Rokin at Spui. The four main concentric canals run parallel to each other as they curve round, linked now and then by small cross-canals.

Singel, the inner canal of the horseshoe, was once the city's fortified boundary, though the wall behind it has long since disappeared. Look out for No. 7, the narrowest house in Amsterdam – it's only as wide as its front door. Three bridges down, at the junction with Oude Leliestraat, note the iron-barred windows of a quaint old jail set into the bridge itself and just above water level. Approachable only by water, it's said to have been used to keep drunks quiet overnight.

Herengracht was *the* fashionable address to have during the city's Golden Age. The wealthiest merchants vied with each other to build the widest homes, the most elaborate gables, the most impressive front entrance steps. The patrician houses are still here in all their glory, though most are now occupied by banks and offices. No. 502, however, is the official residence of the *Burgomaster* (Lord Mayor) of Amsterdam.

Keizersgracht was named after Holy Roman Emperor Maximilian I. The houses on this canal are not quite as grand as on Herengracht, but they are still charming.. Look out for No. 123, the 'House of the Six Heads' (*Huis met de hoofden*). The carved heads are said to represent six burglars who were caught and beheaded by a maid.

Prinsengracht is packed with narrow houses and ware-houses. The original buyers here were mostly traders, and many of the warehouses retain their original appearance. Officially protected from demolition, some have been trans-formed into luxury apartments – in great demand with young executives. The ubiquitous Amsterdam hoisting-beam, once used for goods, still protrudes from the top of most buildings, but nowadays its main use is in getting prosperous owners' new sofas in through the big windows.

All the canals are lined with a splendid variety of façades and gables. Where most houses were narrow (city tax was levied according to size of frontage), the main chance for individuality was the design of the gable. This has become synonymous with 17th-century Dutch architecture (see p.20).

Looking around from your tour boat seat, you'll quickly see that this is a city with more canals than Venice, more bicycles than Copenhagen, and flotillas of houseboats like nowhere else on earth – over 2500 of them from luxury living to simple rafts.

From spring to autumn you might also consider another tour in the late evening, as some of the main canals and bridges are floodlit after dusk.

Another way of using the waterways to see the city is the **Museumboat**, (summer only), which you can hop on and off at points convenient to some of the main museums. A guide and reductions at some of the museums are included.

South-West Section:

VONDELPARK TO MUNTPLEIN

Leidseplein (*plein* = square) is the site of the old city gate on the road to Leiden. Today, the gate, the markets and the carriages have gone, and in their place is a multitude of restaurants, sandwich shops, outdoor cafés, cinemas, discotheques, nightclubs and bars – with several airline offices squeezed in between. There's always a bustle of activity on Leidseplein, one of the city's focal points, with street performers occasionally putting on a show. An ice-hockey rink occupies the middle of the square in winter. Just to the east, Max Euwe Plein boasts a stylish new complex of shops and Amsterdam's only casino (see page 93).

The north-west side of the square is dominated by the **Stadsschouwburg** (Municipal Theatre), with its pillared entrance. Built in 1894, it is home to the Toneelgroep Amsterdam and is host to visiting productions.

The **American Hotel,** near to the theatre, is something of a city tradition. Begun in 1880 and full of character, it has a magnificent Art Nouveau restaurant, protected as an architectural monument. This has long been a very popular meeting place for sightseers, students and anyone who likes to chat and be seen.

Vondelpark, to the south west, is only 200yds (220m) away, This 'lung' for the densely built city centre is named after Holland's foremost poet, Joost van den Vondel. Its 120 acres (296 hectares) include lawns, lakes and flower displays. The park is home to the **Filmmuseum** (three films a day) and in summer it hosts an open-air music and theatre festival.

Nearby **Museumplein,** a broad, grassy square bright with crocuses and daffodils in spring, and a favourite spot for demonstrations, is bordered by three major art museums and the main concert hall.

A landmark on Leidseplein, the Art Nouveau American Hotel, complete with stained glass.

At the city end is the palace-like **Rijksmuseum,** designed by Petrus Cuypers and opened in 1885, home of one of the world's great art collections, including Rembrandt's *The Night Watch.* On the right-hand side of the square, as you look along it from the Rijksmuseum, are the **Vincent van Gogh Museum** designed by Gerrit Rietveld, its glass-box exterior unlike anything else on the square, and the **Stedelijk Museum** containing the city's rich collection of modern art. Most visitors to Amsterdam head for the Rijksmuseum, but art-lovers will not want to miss any of them. For details, see also MUSEUMS, p.48.

The **Royal Concertgebouw** (Concert Hall), at one end of Museumplein, is home to the world-famous orchestra of the same name. Opened in 1888, during a boom in cultural building, it has a main **27** hall which seats 2200 people and is renowned for its nearperfect acoustics.

From here you can make your way back to Leidseplein by going west along Van Baerlestraat and turning right down P.C. Hoofstraat, the two streets which are the focus of Amster-dam's modest centre of *haute couture*. Or head back to the Rijksmuseum through the passageway (often lined by hopeful vendors of crafts and jewellery, and buskers) and then along Nieuwe Spiegelstraat to inspect the numerous **antique shops**.

Bright with flowers by day and lit up at night, the floating flower market (below) spreads along the Singel Canal near the impressive Munttoren (above right), most famous of the many towers in the city.

Starting again from Leidseplein and going north east, you come straight into Leidsestraat, closed to traffic (but watch out for the trams). This was once the top shopping street in town, and you can still find several quality stores along it, amongst all the airline offices and sandwich shops.

Make a point of seeing the **floating flower market** (*drijvende bloemenmarkt*) to the right at the end of Leidsestraat, where it meets the Singel canal. Here, for more than 200 years, Amsterdammers have stepped aboard the gently swaying, floating shop-boats moored at the canalside to buy some of the profusion of plants and flowers that you'll see in the windows of their homes.

Plants overflow onto the canalside over a 200yd (183m) stretch that sometimes resembles a miniature jungle.

The **Munttoren** (Mint Tower) overlooks this colourful and fragrant scene, its 17th-century carillon adding an extra touch of gaiety by chiming out an old Dutch tune every half-hour.

The tower was originally a medieval gate let into the fortified city wall along the Singel canal. Fire destroyed the upper part in 1619, and the present decorative little clock tower was added a year later by Hendrik de Keyser, city architect and best-known stonemason of his day in Holland. In 1672, the Dutch war with France, England, Münster and Cologne temporarily cut off money to Amsterdam, and the city began to mint its own in this building. The name has remained ever since. **29**

North-West Section:

KALVERSTRAAT AND DAM SQUARE TO JORDAAN

The brasher face of Amsterdam retailing is found along Kalverstraat, running north from Munttoren to the short, broad street called Spui, not to be confused with nearby Spuistraat. (Ask a Dutch person how to pronounce the name: you certainly won't get it right otherwise.)

Across the street and to the left, hidden behind an arched oak doorway, lies one of the city's great surprises, a haven of tranquillity known as the **Begijnhof** (Beguine Court). Neat lawns are surrounded by perfect 17th- and 18th-century alms-houses, two small churches and a wooden house dating from 1477. English Pilgrim Fathers who fled to Holland before joining the *Mayflower* prayed regularly in the church of the Beguine Court which **30** dates originally from 1392 and

has been known since 1607 as the Scottish Presbyterian Church. Opposite is the Catholic church which nuns installed in two of the almshouses during the Calvinist domination of Amsterdam in the 17th century. One of its fine stained-glass windows commemorates the 'wafer miracle' of 1345 (see p.13).

The court was originally founded in 1346 for the benefit of the Beguines, members of a Dutch lay sisterhood. Today, the Beguine Court's houses are occupied at a nominal rent, mostly by elderly ladies, although some are now let to younger ones. Leaving the Beguine Court through the Civic Guard Gallery, lined with 17th century portraits, you come to the **Amsterdams Historisch Museum** (Amsterdam Historical Museum), newly restored after serving as an orphanage for almost 400 years. Its many

*T*he Royal (Koninklijk) Palace dominating Dam Square is now only used for state receptions.

rooms and galleries tell the city's story from 1275 to present day, with exhibits ranging from prehistoric remains and the city's original charter to audio-visual slide shows on land reclamation. Don't miss the St. Luciënsteeg entrance, where 22 old city gablestones have been restored and set into the wall.

If you leave by the Kalverstraat exit, you can continue north, in the company of the bustling shopping crowds on this pedestrian-only street, to Amsterdam's main square.

Dam Square (simply Dam in Dutch) is the city's heart and *raison d'être*, a no-frills area always throbbing with life. It was here that the River Amstel was dammed some time before 1275, eventually to be filled in completely along Damrak and Rokin.

Dam Square is dominated by the **Koninklijk Paleis** (Royal Palace) opened as the Town Hall in 1655 at the height of the halcyon Golden Age. It was converted into a palace by Louis Bonaparte, Napoléon's brother, during his

*T*he impressive interior of the Nieuwe Kerk (left) and (right) the crowned bell-tower of the fine, neo-classic Westerkerk soars graciously above Prinsengracht.

François and Pierre Hemony. At the back of the palace, facing Raadhuisstraat, is a particularly striking statue of Atlas carrying a huge globe. The palace's interior is well worth a visit (see MUSEUMS, p.48).

Just across the narrow Mozes en Aäronstraat stands the **Nieuwe Kerk** (New Church). This simple, late-Gothic basilica, whose origins date back to the 15th century, was built without a tower (the neo-Gothic steeple adorning it today was added in the mid-19th century). The rather stark effect inside is relieved by baroque wood-carving and the fine 16th- and 17th-century organs. An extensive programme of restoration was carried out during the 1970s and it is now often used for exhibitions and meetings.

brief sojourn in Amsterdam when the Emperor installed him as King of Holland (1806-10). Today Queen Beatrix uses the palace only to welcome visiting dignitaries and for state receptions, preferring to live in the Huis ten Bosch on the outskirts of The Hague. The Dam Palace fronts straight onto the busy and often noisy square. Above the wide gable of the tympanum stands a Virgin of Peace statue and, behind her, the domed carillon bell tower (still playing tunes to the crowds below), installed by the

32 famous campanologist brothers

Many statesmen and heroes are buried in the Nieuwe Kerk (for example Admiral de Ruyter, in an ornate tomb near the high altar, and the poet Joost van den Vondel), and The Netherlands' monarchs are sworn in here.

The white, stone column on the other side of the square is the **National Monument**, paid for by subscription and erected in 1956 to commemorate the Dutch role in World War II. In a small curved wall at the back of the monument there are 12 urns – 11 filled with soil from each Dutch province, and the twelfth with soil from Indonesia.

Madame Tussaud's, a branch of the London waxworks, is housed above a department store on the Dam. You emerge from the lift to meet a moving, talking 15ft (4.5m) giant personification of 17th-century Holland who greets you and sends you on your way through scenes from Dutch history, naturally including Rembrandt in his studio. You'll find yourself in sets inspired by Vermeer paintings,

or mingling with Dutch soccer stars, comedians, and singers as well as more familiar waxwork figures, some more lifelike than others.

Behind the Koninklijk Paleis, Raadhuisstraat leads to **Westerkerk** (West Church) on the Keizersgracht. Begun in 1619 by Hendrik de Keyser and finished in neo-classical style after his death by Jacob van Campen, it is distinguished not only by its tower – Amsterdam's tallest at 273ft (83m) – but also by the shining, multicoloured crown with an orb on top, a replica of the crown presented to the city by Holy Roman Emperor Maximilian I in 1489.

The interior is spacious, but Calvinistically spartan in atmosphere. The organ was added in the 1680s, its panels painted by de Lairesse, a pupil of Rembrandt. A plaque on the north wall records the fact that Rembrandt himself was buried in the church, but exactly where he lies is not known.

Energetic visitors can climb the tower (in summer only) for an incomparable **view** of the city. Aloft, the carillon of 47 bells, some cast by François Hemony, strikes out merry tunes each half-hour of the day *and* night. If you're staying in a hotel nearby, you'll remember the tunes for years.

The **Anne Frankhuis** (Anne Frank House) is just around the corner at Prinsengracht 263. In this building, dating from 1635, you can see the rooms where the young Jewish girl and her family hid from the occupying Nazi forces between 1942 and 1944. (To understand how it was possible, collect the leaflet with its cutaway diagram of the building as you enter.)

At the top of the steep stairway you can still see the bookcase wall which seems to close off a corridor, but which in fact swings out and gives access to the secret *achterhuis*, or concealed part of the house behind. Here Anne, her family and four friends eked out an existence until they were betrayed just nine months before the war ended. The stove they used is still there, as well as poignant magazine cuttings of Anne's favourite stars, stuck on the wall by this 15-year-old who did not survive.

Anne Frank and her sister died in Bergen-Belsen in 1945, a week before the liberation. But she left an incomparable diary for the world, published by her father, the only survivor of the eight. Since it first appeared in 1947, more than 14 million copies in 50 languages have been printed. Always thronging with visitors, the house is open from Monday to Saturday, 9 a.m. to 5 p.m.; Sunday 10 a.m. to 5 p.m.

The **Jordaan** area, across the canal, lies between the west bank of the Prinsengracht and the Lijnbaansgracht and extends north-south roughly from the Haarlemmerdijk to the Leidsegracht. Its name may be derived from the French word *jardin* (garden) – many Huguenot refugees from France lived here at one time. All its streets and canals are named after trees and flowers (Lindenstraat, Rozengracht, Bloemgracht etc.), but it was certainly not laid out as a leafy garden suburb back in the early 17th century. It was, in fact, a poor relation of the central merchant canals, a poor working-class area overcrowded with small homes and narrow streets.

Today it has become a sought-after area for artists and designers. The 'garden' has blossomed with a variety of small shops, boutiques and restaurants alongside the area's traditional 'brown cafés' (see EATING OUT, p.109). Many of its 8000 houses are designated as protected monuments. Several cheerful children's playgrounds have been created in the dense backstreets of the Jordaan. Being a vivacious, off-beat, charming area, it holds a slightly crazy festival of its own in September (see p. 95).

The **Koepelzaal** (formerly the Ronde Lutherse Kerk) is located on the Singel canal. Its 146ft (44.5m)-high copper dome has dominated the old herring-packers' quarters here since 1671. It was built in baroque style, using two million bricks and 3615 piles, and the copper for the dome was donated by devout Lutheran King Charles XI of Sweden and allowed into the city duty free. The church was rebuilt after being gutted by fire in 1822, and in 1830 a handsome organ was installed.

Over the next century, however, congregations dwindled to such an extent that in 1935 the church was de-consecrated and for a while was used as a warehouse. In the 1970s, however, came a surprise new lease of life. An American hotel chain began to convert a cluster of 17th-century houses into a modern hotel and, along with the city authorities and **35** the Dutch National Monuments Committee, restored the round Lutheran Church opposite into an annexe now used as a grand banqueting hall and reception/conference area.

Organ concerts are normally held on Sunday mornings under the 62ft (19m) diameter dome. However, these are not taking place at the moment, as fire struck the church again in 1993, resulting in severe damage to the organ and parts of the building. Restoration work is currently being carried out, so check with the local tourist office for details of reopening.

For a change of perspective, go north along the Singel and under the railway to the Havengebouw (harbour building) just west of the railway station. From the top of the building there is a superb **panoramic view** over the whole of Amsterdam. And if you feel in need of refreshment after sightseeing, there's also a rooftop restaurant.

Central Section:

DAMRAK TO WATERLOOPLEIN

Railway stations are rarely tourist sights, but the **Centraal Station,** which dominates the Damrak boulevard vista, is a considerable engineering feat and a fine 19th century neo-Gothic monument. It was built by Petrus Cuypers, architect also of the Rijksmuseum, to which the station bears obvious resemblances, on three artificial islands and 8,687 wooden piles.

On the waterfront opposite the station and now housing the VVV tourist office and a restaurant, the NZH (Noord-Zuid Hollands) Koffiehuis had to be rebuilt in 1981 – the authorities pulled down the original 1911 building during the construction of the metro.

*H*ouseboats along Singel Canal and the magnificent dome of Koepelzaal.

Diagonally opposite the station to the left is the charming **St.-Nicolaaskerk** (St. Nicholas' Church), where the Dutch counterpart to Santa Claus comes ceremonially ashore to make his entry into the city in the weeks before Christmas.

Just a few yards down Damrak from Centraal Station, the **Beurs van Berlage (**formerly the Stock Exchange building), designed by Hendrik Petrus Berlage, has always excited controversy. It was one of Berlage's ultra-modern masterpieces when first unveiled to the world in 1903. Now it serves as a concert hall, home of the Netherlands Philharmonic Orchestra. Architectural exhibits are on show here as well.

The **Oude Kerk** (Old Church) is to be found just behind Beursplein and across Warmoesstraat. Amsterdam's oldest and biggest church, it was consecrated around 1300 and largely completed by 1400. Never burned down or badly damaged, its interior is the most impressive of the city's churches. Rembrandt's wife **37**

Saskia is buried here: a simple stone engraved with her name forms part of the floor under the small organ. Though a wealth of decoration and statuary was disposed of by 17th-century Calvinists as 'Catholic pomp', there remains plenty of Gothic stone carving worthy of admiration both inside and out, as well as some fine stained-glass including a window commemorating the Peace of Westphalia which, with the Peace of The Hague, brought an end to the 80-year Spanish War in 1648.

Practically filling its own small square, the Old Church is surrounded by Amsterdam's **red-light district**. This area, popularly known in Dutch as the *walletjes* or 'little walls', is concentrated along Warmoesstraat, Oudezijds Voorburgwal, Oudezijds Achterburgwal and Zeedijk, where sex shops, live sex shows and sex 'museums' have mushroomed in recent years. It's perfectly safe to stroll around – except perhaps in the early hours – and has become a prime tourist attraction. The ladies in the windows

*O*ne of the oldest (and once most fashionable) parts of the city is now the inescapably bizarre 'red light district'.

will ignore you, unless you take an obvious interest. It's quite typical of Amsterdam that plenty of ordinary businesses, shops, houses and restaurants are dotted throughout the area as well – and you'll likewise spot red lights glowing in side streets in other parts of the city.

Museum Amstelkring, otherwise known as *Ons 'Lieve Heer Op Solder* (Our Lord in the Attic Church), at Oudezijds Voorburgwal 40, is the only one of Amsterdam's 60 once-clandestine Catholic churches of the Calvinist era left in the original condition. Tucked away up a series of steep stairs and winding corridors, you'll find numerous relics of interest from the 18th century before reaching the beautiful church itself. (See also MUSEUMS, p.56.)

Cross the small Chinese quarter of the lower Zeedijk to reach the **Schreierstoren,** dating from 1482. There is some dispute over whether the tower's name derives from an old word meaning 'to cry out', or from another word meaning 'astride'. Certainly the tower was built astride the Geldersekade canal as a fortification on the old city harbour wall, but it was also the point of departure for sailors, and the legend of the Weeping Tower, or Tower of Tears, has a more romantic appeal. It was from here that Henry Hudson left to discover Manhattan in 1609, and two plaques on the tower commemorate the event, one of them presented by the Port of New York 350 years later.

Just within sight of Schreierstoren you'll probably have spotted the three masts of a great sailing ship, the *Amsterdam*. She's moored at the quayside as part of the collection of the **Nederlands Scheepvaartmuseum** (Netherlands' Maritime Museum), appropriately commanding a panoramic view of the harbour.

39

Separate from the floating exhibits, the museum itself is housed in a vast old Admiralty supply building called 's Lands Zeemagazijn, dating from 1656, and now full of model ships, charts, instruments and all the fascinating paraphernalia of sailing. (See also MUSEUMS, p.54.)

The **Montelbaanstoren** (Montelbaan Tower), on the Oude Schans canal where it meets Oude Waal, is said to be the city's best-proportioned

tower. It was built as part of the 15th-century defences and bristled with cannon on its then flat roof. In 1606, Hendrik de Keyser added the present 143ft (44m) spire, with clock and bells, in the same neo-classical style as his other towers. A question you might like to consider is whether it is the tower that leans, or the nearby house – or both.

The **Waag** (Weigh House) stands like a medieval, seven-turreted castle on Nieuwmarkt square. It was built in 1488 as a city gate, but as such was little used. It has had a varied career as weigh-house, fire station, guildhouse, museum and information centre, and currently awaits restoration amid predictable controversy about what should be done with the building.

Guilds which once met here included (among others) the stonemasons, who left samples of their skill on both the outside and the inside. Amsterdam's surgeons' guild held weekly anatomy lessons here in the 17th century and invited Rembrandt along to record the scene. The results were his two now world-famous paintings, both entitled *The Anatomy Lesson* (one of *Dr. Tulp*, the other of *Dr. Deijman*). All the guilds using the Weigh House had their own doorways, which remain dotted around in an apparent confusion of entrances.

Nearby **Zuiderkerk** (South Church) was the first church to be built in the city after the Reformation and has an appropriately simple interior. It was constructed between 1603 and 1611 by de Keyser (who is buried here). He added the tower in 1614, which was so admired by Christopher Wren,

Landmarks in the oldest part of the city: the former defence post Montelbaanstoren (left) and the strange Waag, once a city gate.

it's said to have been the proto-type for some of his famous London spires. Another noted figure inspired to sketch and paint it – Rembrandt van Rijn – who lived opposite. Now de-consecrated, the church is home to the information centre of the city planning depart-ment, and the focus for heated debate every time a scheme for urban renewal is proposed.

Across the Oude Schans canal, Jodenbreestraat (Jewish Broad Street) is a reminder that until World War II this was part of the old Jewish quarter. The **Rembrandthuis** (Rembrandt's House) at Jodenbreestraat 4-6, red-shuttered and three storeys high, is a 1606 brick building with a stepped gable. It was the home of Holland's greatest painter from 1639 until his bankruptcy in 1660. Rem-brandt lived initially in grand style here, aided by his wife Saskia's 40,000-guilder dowry but also painting prolifically in an attempt to pay his way. Many of his finest works date from this period, including the *Anatomy Lesson of Dr. Deijman*, *The Night Watch* and

The classical façade of the Moses and Aaron church faces Waterlooplein.

The Polish Rider. (See also MUSEUMS, p.57)

The end of Jodenbreestraat is dominated by the **Mozes en Aäronkerk** (Moses and Aaron Church), a Catholic church built in 1840 with an imposing classical façade and a pillared entrance surmounted by a statue of Christ, and twin towers at each end of the balustraded roof. Two gable-stones of 'Moyses' and 'Aaron' from an earlier church on this site are set into the wall.

Its colourful, baroque-like interior looks down today on scenes never envisaged by the church's founders. A meeting place for travelling youth, where they can buy soft drinks and snacks, or stage art and craft exhibitions, it has also become a centre for foreign workers who come here to attend their own special Sun-day services.

South-East Section:

WATERLOOPLEIN TO OOSTERPARK

In front of the Moses and Aaron church, the once vast open space known as **Waterlooplein** has been greatly reduced since the building of the brick-and-glass **Muziektheater** (Music Theatre) which opened in 1986. The 1600-seat theatre is home to the Netherlands Opera and the National Ballet. Because the complex also includes the city's town hall (*stadhuis*), Amsterdammers have created the nickname *Stopera* (*stadhuis + opera*).

Amsterdam's **flea-market** on Waterlooplein spreads into the neighbouring streets and round the Muziektheater. The cheery stallholders will gaily sell you anything from a twisted piece of lead piping to a fine old wind-up gramophone, a cheap modern lock, a solid oak table, outboard motor, century-old doll or a new shirt.

43

It's all bustle and bonhomie, with hardly any prices marked. No matter what language you use to ask the price, the vendors' answers will be anything up to twice what they are eventually willing to take. This is one place in the city where you can really haggle. If you can't come to an agreement, however, don't expect to be called back. Your good-natured stallholder will by this time have turned into a typical stubborn Amsterdammer who would rather lose cash than face.

Across Visserplein from the Moses and Aaron church, the **Portugees-Israëlitische Synagoge** (Portuguese synagogue) was built in 1675 by the then-large community of Sephardic Jews, descendants of late 16th-century refugees from Spain and Portugal. It's said to have been patterned on the plan of King Solomon's temple. (The synagogue, on Jonas Daniël Meijer Square, is open irregularly.)

Adjoining the synagogue, the Ets Haim 'Tree of Life' library, dating from 1616, con-

tains 20,000 books, prints and rare manuscripts highlighting Jewish history.

The **Jewish Historical Museum** (see also MUSEUMS, p.56) also faces the square, housed in the restored Great Synagogue (1670).

Here, too, you'll see the **Dockworker Statue** by Mari Andriessen. Revered by Amsterdam's Jews and non-Jews alike, this rough figure of a man in working clothes commemorates the events of February 1941, when Amsterdam's dockworkers staged a courageous 24-hour strike in protest against the deportation of the Jews by the occupying Nazi forces.

The River Amstel, from which Amsterdam takes its name, is only a minute's walk away. For the best river view in town, cross the **Blauwbrug** (Blue Bridge). Built in the 1880s and named after a former blue-painted wooden drawbridge on the same site, it is a copy of the Pont Alexandre III in Paris and is richly ornamented with golden crowns and ships' prows.

Some consider it the city's most beautiful bridge, but look along the river to see its immediate rival, the white wooden drawbridge with nine graceful arches, the **Magere Brug**, or 'Skinny Bridge', as it can be colloquially translated. It's a bottleneck for the single-file traffic but a delight for photographers, especially in summer at dusk when, outlined with electric lights, it throws a perfect mirror-image onto the still water. By day at all times of the year the Skinny Bridge is regularly raised and lowered to allow passage to the busy barge traffic.

The name Magere is doubly significant: the bridge is indeed narrow, and *magere* in Dutch means thin or meagre, but a previous 17th-century bridge on this site is said to have been paid for by two sisters, coincidentally called Magere, who lived nearby.

Just beyond the Magere Brug, the riverside **Theater Carré** is an attractive white-stone building dating from 1887. Generally, it features Dutch-language shows, but there are also occasional performances by visiting theatre, dance and pop groups from abroad.

The gardens of the **Willet Holthuysen Museum** are on your left as you walk down Amstelstraat. Like the museum itself (the entrance is on

M agere Brug across the River Amstel stars in countless visitors' photographs.

45

parallel Herengracht – see also MUSEUMS, p.56), they are in authentic 17th- and 18th-century style.

Rembrandtsplein (Rembrandt Square) and the adjoining Thorbeckeplein are a scaled-down version of Times Square in New York, or Leicester Square in London. Covered with advertising, cinema, restaurant, bar and nightclub signs, they form a brash, fun area offering everything from strip-shows and English-language films to a cup of coffee at one of the many outdoor cafés. The green centre of the square, complete with benches, is a pleasant relief from the frenzy all around, particularly when the banks of rhododendrons are out in full bloom.

Utrechtsestraat, leading south out of the square, especially Reguliersdwarsstraat, to the west, have major concentrations of **restaurants** of every variety. There's a **view** of 14 bridges from the far end of Thorbeckeplein. Look along Reguliersgracht to see six of them in a row. To the left down

*A*n oasis of peace and calm in the middle of brash, commercial Rembrandtsplein.

Herengracht are six more, and to the right another two. It's a particularly memorable sight in summer after dark, when all the bridges are lit.

South-Eastern Parks and Gardens

Three distinctive patches of green might entice you to extend your tour of the southeast part of the city, or to make a special expedition (take tram route 9).

Behind the Portuguese synagogue, along Muiderstraat and across Nieuwe Herengracht, you'll find yourself in **Hortus Botanicus**, the lush botanical gardens and greenhouses of the University of Amsterdam. They were started centuries ago by a group of monks who introduced thousands of exotic species for medicinal use.

Artis, nearby on Plantage Middenlaan, houses Amsterdam's **Zoo**, set up in 1838 – one of the earliest in Europe. In fact it's much more than a zoo, and includes a large aquarium, a planetarium and a new geological museum, all in an informal atmosphere. You can approach the animals as closely as safety allows and great efforts have been made to give them plenty of space, light and air, although some of the big cats are still confined in a way that many people find increasingly unacceptable.

Across two canals to the south east of Artis, **Oosterpark** is another of the city's welcome green expanses, with lakes and plenty of play areas. On its northern edge, the **Tropenmuseum** (Tropical Museum) was once just a conventional collection of ethnographic material gathered together from The Netherlands' colonial territories. Now, it's an innovative and exciting place, housed in a palatial, late-19th century, galleried building (see also MUSEUMS, p.57).

47

Museums

Amsterdam's museums are generally open from 10 or 11 a.m. to 5 p.m. on weekdays (some close on Mondays) and from 1 to 5 p.m. on Sundays and public holidays.

Admission prices range from moderate to high by international standards. A special one-year ticket (*Museumjaarkaart*) for all state museums in The Netherlands as well as the municipal museums in Amsterdam is available at most VVV Tourist Information Offices and major museums on presentation of your passport and a photograph. If you plan to make more than about five museum visits during the year, this ticket represents quite a substantial saving.

To combine a trip on the water with a visit to a museum, there is a canalboat service which stops at the main museums (see also p.25).

Remember that The Netherlands designates what Americans call the first floor the *ground* floor, the second floor the *first* floor, and so on.

THE BIG THREE

Rijksmuseum

Fortunately for bewildered visitors to this vast, 250-room, museum, a clear ground plan, with an index of exhibits, is included with your ticket at the kiosk outside the main door.

If your main interest is European art, and Dutch painting in particular, head for rooms 201-236 on the first floor. Tour groups and others who are short of time or only want to see a few highlights will cut through to the long central gallery, subdivided into rooms 229-236 with, at the far end, room 224, the site of Rembrandt's monumental work, *The Night Watch* (properly entitled *The Company of Captain Frans Banning Cocq and Lieutenant Willem van Ruytenburch*).

Painted in 1642, when the artist was 37, it broke radically from traditional group portraits in that the figures were not lined up in formal rows or seated stiffly like a sports team in an old photograph. Also

*C*ome face to face with those famous Dutch Masters in the Rijksmuseum.

evident is the interplay of light and shadow which was such a revolutionary element in Rembrandt's work. Indeed, some of the members of Amsterdam's Civic Guard who had commissioned *The Night Watch*, and whom it portrays, may well have been surprised by its unconventional composition. But the story that they tucked it away on one of the least favourable walls of their new meeting hall, or even refused to accept it, are dismissed by experts these days as groundless myth.

Other highlights among the Rembrandt works on display include the lustrous and tender *Loving Couple* (also called *The Jewish Bride)*, the slightly comic *Self-Portrait as the Apostle Paul*, for which he donned a turban, and the *Staalmeesters*, (1662) a late work which confirmed him **49** again as one of the greatest group portrait painters the world has ever known.

A special luminosity marks the tantalizingly small number of surviving works by another great original of the Netherlands' Golden Age, Jan Vermeer (1632–75). Nowhere is this better seen than in his *Young Woman Reading a Letter*, one of four of his works on display here.

Portraits by Frans Hals (1580–1666) include his superb *The Merry Drinker*. Look out also for the pale, glowing church interiors which were the speciality of Saenredam (1597–1665).

Jacob van Ruisdael (1628–82), is often considered the greatest landscape painter of his century. His work is represented here by, among others, the *Mill near Wijk bij Duurstede* and *View of Haarlem*. These, and the idealized landscapes of Albert Cuyp (1620–91) met the challenge of making a convincing picture of the flat Dutch terrain. You'll appreciate the achievement more if you have tried photograph-ing similar scenes and only ended up with a long low line.

Jan Steen (1626–79), in contrast to the formal portraits commissioned by the wealthy, painted often hilarious observations of village life and family feastings.

The Rijksmuseum also has works by many non-Dutch artists, although rarely more than one or two by each are on show. Check the plan and gallery list that comes with your ticket or ask at the information desk if you want to see pictures by Rubens, Botticelli, Fra Angelico, Tintoretto, El Greco, Goya and Velázquez.

To give more than a very general idea of the other varied treasures that the Rijksmuseum contains is impossible here. Whether your interests extend to porcelain, Asiatic art, Dutch history and furniture, 18th-century glassware or 17th-century dolls' houses, to name but a few of the other exhibits, the Rijksmuseum has something for you. There is a fine shop and also a café.

Location: Stadhouderskade 42. (Closed on Monday.)

✓ Stedelijk Museum

The Stedelijk's collection of famous names is as impressive, in its own field, as that of the Rijksmuseum. Displayed in wonderfully lit, spacious galleries, Picasso is represented by *Still Life with Guitar, Glass with Straws* and *Sitting Woman with Fish Hat*. Works by Monet, Degas, Cézanne and Matisse are here along with many works by the two Dutch artists Piet Mondrian and Willem de Kooning. But look especially for Chagall. His *Pregnant Woman* and *Man with Violin* are unforgettably serio-comic and colourful. There's also a wide range of works by the Russian, Casimir Malevich, and other innovators including Rothko and Lichtenstein. Special exhibitions are constantly being mounted, and the Stedelijk's wide-ranging taste embraces most things from trans to Andy Warhol. There's a good museum shop and café.

Location: Paulus Potterstraat 13 (on Museumplein). (Open 11 a.m. to 5 p.m. daily.)

Vincent van Gogh Museum

This modern, 1973 building houses in its open-galleried interior over 200 paintings and 400 drawings by van Gogh (1853–90), plus a room of works by contemporaries such as Toulouse-Lautrec, Monet, Daumier, Corot and Vincent's sometime friend, Gauguin.

A few sketches survive from his London days where as a young man he worked as an apprentice to a Dutch art dealer, fell in love, and despaired when he was jilted. After studying in Brussels and The Hague, he moved to a village in Brabant in 1884, intending to share the life of the rural poor. This period resulted in the brooding landscapes, dark still-lifes and lamp-lit peasant scenes which make up this chronologically arranged collection, including his first masterpiece, *The Potato Eaters* (1885).

Moving to Antwerp and on to Paris (where he painted no fewer than 11 self-portraits, when he was too poor to pay **51** models), he encountered the latest trends in French art and became excited by brilliant colour. In search of an environment to match, he went south to Arles, where he painted in a compulsive frenzy during 1888 and 1889, producing many of the works on view here; his series of blossom paintings, wheatfields and harvest scenes, orchards and sunflowers.

After a breakdown, he moved to a mental clinic at Saint Rémy, where he remembered his bedroom at Arles, and this is one of the more famous works on display, among other electrifying images from the year of his death. Notice also his re-workings of works by such masters as Rembrandt, Délacroix and Millet.

Apart from his canvases and a gallery of painted Japanese woodcuts, an art form which he much admired, the museum also houses hundreds of letters from Vincent, his family and friends. This collection was begun by Vincent's younger brother Theo, his greatest supporter, who unfortunately survived him by only six months. (Open 11 a.m. to 5 p.m. daily.)
Location: Paulus Potterstraat 7 (on Museumplein).

Amsterdams Historisch Museum

Housed in a charmingly restored 17th-century orphanage and ranged around a succession of courtyards in the heart of the city. Classic Dutch paintings are to be found here too, but in the main this is a rich and beautifully arranged record of Amsterdam's history from 1275 to 1945.
Location: Kalverstraat 92. See also p. 30.

Aviodome

Inside a dome which looks quite small from the outside but houses many full-size aircraft, you can follow a clockwise path through the whole history of aviation. Beginning with the 18th-century Montgolfier hot-air balloon, exhibits move chronologically starting with the Wright brothers, then World

52

Dutch Masters, Old and New

FRANS HALS (c. 1580-1666) is often considered the founder of the Dutch School. He is famous for portraits and groups. *The Laughing Cavalier* and *The Merry Drinker* (in the Rijksmuseum) demonstrate his gift for giving subjects a lively air.

REMBRANDT HARMENSZ VAN RIJN (1606-69) is the undisputed giant of Dutch painting. Born in Leiden, he acquired fame and fortune (before becoming bankrupt) in Amsterdam. His revolutionary use of light and shade, and genius in group portraits, is seen in *The Night Watch*. Of 600 works once accepted as being by Rembrandt, only 300 passed the scrutiny of modern science and scholarship (much to the chagrin of the owners of the others).

JACOB VAN RUISDAEL (c. 1628-82) is the great master of the landscape. He's known for the vivid scenes he painted of his native Haarlem, as true to life as a photograph.

JAN VERMEER (1632-75) was born and died in Delftt. His fame is based upon a known output of only about 30 paintings, celebrated for their delicate interiors, and for the air of mystery surrounding the characters portrayed.

VINCENT VAN GOGH (1853-90) was apprenticed to an art dealer based in The Hague.. Disillusioned with this, he began to train as a teacher in England before becoming aware of his creative powers as an artist. He worked without recognition in Antwerp and Paris before spending most of his last two years in Arles. His art is inseparable from his tormented inner life.

PIET MONDRIAAN, or Mondrian (1872-1944) spent many years in Paris before moving to London, Arizona and New York, where he died. His abstract paintings, consisting often of stark rectangles in primary colours, represent the reduction of a subject to its most basic, underlying essence.

WILLEM DE KOONING, born in Rotterdam in 1904, settled in the United States in 1926, where he developed his own brand of abstract expressionism, notably in the lurid *Woman* series.

War I and a replica of the Fokker Triplane, a World War II Spitfire Mark 9, and a DC-3, followed by the early years of KLM in the 1920s. Children can try the small flight simulators. (Open daily.)

Location: Schiphol Airport.

Bijbels Museum

(Biblical Museum and Workshop)

In two houses dating from 1662, a Judaeo-Christian exhibition aims to show what it was like to live in Palestine around the time of Christ. Other exhibits include Middle East archaeological finds and early printed bibles. In the workshop, children are encouraged to paint, draw, make models, play musical instruments and act out plays on biblical themes. (Closed Monday.)

Location: Herengracht 368.

Stichting de Appel

Formerly the Institute of Contemporary Art, this site has been taken over by the Appel foundation. A stark, challenging space has been created inside the shell of several old buildings in the middle of the 'antiques district'. Its modernity complements the latest ideas in art shown in frequently changing displays. Open Tuesday through Sunday.

Location: Nieuwe Spiegelstraat 10.

Nederlands Scheepvaartmuseum

(Netherlands Maritime Museum).

The prize exhibit is a superb full-size replica of the 17th century ship *Amsterdam*, afloat in the quayside next to the museum. Costumed characters welcome you aboard and explain what life was like on the long voyage to the east and back.

Inside the museum itself, the several hundred detailed models mostly date from the same period as the ships they depict. Paintings, prints, countless historic maps, charts, globes, pilot books and a library of 60,000 volumes – many from the 16th and 17th

54

centuries – evoke the time when the Dutch were the world's greatest maritime power. Look for the certificate of purchase that American Indians gave to Dutch merchant Peter Minuit for land around Albany, New York, in 1631, and the oldest known depiction of New York City, 1656.

The upper floors cover the modern era, with more models and actual examples of many smaller vessels right up to today's pleasure craft. (Closed Monday, mid Sept–mid June.) *Location:* Kattenburgerplein 1. See also p. 39.

*R*eplica Dutch East Indiaman the Amsterdam moored at the Sceepvaartmuseum.

Koninklijk Paleis
(Royal Palace)
The huge, classic interior of this 17th-century town hall, which became a royal residence, contains a mass of sculpted symbolism by Artus Quellinus the Elder and others, and some of the finest Empire furniture in the world, left behind by Louis Bonaparte when he fled **55**

the city overnight in 1810 (see p.31). In the massive 97ft (29m)-high Civic Hall, Quellinus's work looks down on an inlaid mosaic floor of celestial and terrestrial globes fit for a king. Paintings include contributions by Ferdinand Bol, one of Rembrandt's pupils, and works by artist Govert Flinck. *Hours:* (provided the palace is not in use, which it may well be) summer months: 1 p.m. to 5 p.m. daily. Winter months: guided tour Wednesday at 2 p.m. See also p. 31.
Location: Dam Square.

Joods Historisch Museum

(Jewish Historical Museum) Housed in the restored complex of four Ashkenazi synagogues, is this impressive collection of holy Jewish objects, as well as a record of the Second World War occupation. In keeping, the coffee shop serves Jewish culinary specialities. (Open daily 11 a.m. to 5 p.m.)
Location: Jonas Daniël Meijerplein 2–4.

Museum Amstelkring

(also known as *Ons' Lieve Heer Op Solder*, meaning 'Our Lord in the Attic').
This clandestine Catholic church from the Calvinist era occupies the top floor of three 1661–63 homes in one of the most colourful parts of the city. The elegant, balconied church has a 1794 organ which is still used at weddings and a hinged pulpit which can be tucked away out of sight to save space. Other rooms house antiques. (Open daily.)
Location: Oudezijds Voorburgwal 40. See also p.39.

Museum Willet Holthuysen

Built in 1689 as a private residence for an eminent *burgher*, this house still has a family atmosphere and great authenticity. It is, in many respects, a perfect example of a patrician Amsterdam house. Gracious rooms house a fine family collection of art, ceramics and furniture. (Open daily.)
Location: Herengracht 605.

Rembrandthuis

(Rembrandt's House)
The painter's home from 1639–60, a period in which he went from fame to bankruptcy, was restored in his memory in 1906. The chief exhibits are examples of 250 of his etchings (some in various different states) out of fewer than 300 that are known, including many of the most famous of these miniature masterpieces. Rembrandt himself executed all stages of the process, which is clearly explained here. His own etching press is also on display. (Open daily.)
Location: Jodenbreestraat 4–6.
See also p.42.

Six Collectie

(The Six Collection)
An impressive private collection of 17th-century works of art, belonging to the Six family. Jan Six's portrait by his friend, Rembrandt, is a magnificent portrait painted in 1654 and a major part of the collection. To gain entry you must first make a reservation (for which you need your passport) by contacting the Rijksmuseum (see p.48).
Location: Amstel 218.

Tropenmuseum

(Tropical Museum)
In a remarkable, renovated, 19th-century building, this exceptional museum displays the folk art, costumes, and way of life of the peoples of Africa, the Middle East, India, Latin America and especially South-East Asia.

Unlike most ethnographic museums, however, the exhibits are adventurously presented through vivid recreations such as an Arab souk, an Indian town, a Peruvian village. A children's section is guaranteed to fascinate younger visitors, but the whole place is so lively that they should like the main parts too.

Most Sunday afternoons, the museum sponsors free performances of folk song, dance and drama from various parts of the tropical world. (Open daily.)
Location: Linnaeusstraat 2.

Excursions

Amsterdam is the capital of a small country, and it's possible to leave the city behind in ten minutes. Your first windmill will probably soon appear and, when you get on to a secondary road, you'll catch your first glimpse of a farmer – or more likely, a tourist – cycling along wearing wooden yellow shoes.

Within an hour you can get to many other major Dutch cities: for example The Hague is 35 miles (57 km) away, Haarlem 12 miles (19 km), Delft 38 miles (61 km), and Rotterdam 45 miles (73 km).

Several bus companies run a series of well-organized daily excursions, at fair prices which are kept down by competition. If your hotel doesn't have their brochures, you'll find them at the VVV Tourist Office opposite Centraal Station.

Efficient, clean, frequent and reasonably priced trains run to all main towns. Or, if you're motorized and prefer to go it alone, you may like to choose from the excursions in the following pages which introduce some of the different faces of Holland.

Many interesting towns are within easy reach of Amsterdam but outside the scope of this book. Among them, Rotterdam is a phoenix-like city risen from the ashes of the Second World War. From its generously laid-out traffic-free shopping precincts to the dizzying heights of the 600ft (185m)-high Euromast with its view of the huge, bustling port, Rotterdam symbolizes the will not only to survive adversity but also to thrive. Such hallmarks of Dutch determination can be seen everywhere.

BY THE SHORES OF THE IJSSELMEER

(The old Zuider Zee was renamed the IJsselmeer after completion of the barrier dam which cut it off from the North Sea.)

Head north from Amsterdam by the IJ-tunnel, and within ten minutes you can turn off to the left into the utter calm of **Broek in Waterland**.

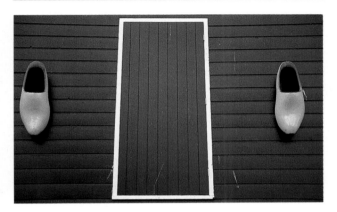

With its narrow streets and wooden houses (as distinct from the red-brick homes usually found in Holland), its tiny lake and profusion of waterfowl, this claims (among many others!) to be the prettiest Dutch village.

Marken, six miles (10 km) to the east, is a former island now linked to the mainland by a causeway. A Calvinist village that strictly keeps the Sabbath, its distinctive local costume is still widely worn. The village has a colourful and genuine old harbour and houses painted green and white or pitch black.

In the old days, houses had signs, not numbers. Here at Marken, some still do.

In spite of its popularity with the tourists, Marken has preserved much of its authenticity and charm.

Back on the mainland, you will soon reach **Monnick-endam**, a former Zuider Zee harbour with a colourful modern port, an impressive late-Gothic church with stained-glass windows, a slender 16th- **59** century tower with carillon and a variety of 17th-century gabled houses.

Next stop is **Volendam**, a much larger Catholic counterpart to Marken, visible across the water. The harbour and main street on top of the dike are lined with souvenir shops and snack bars and crowded with visitors looking for costumed locals to photograph and be photographed with. You can even hire a costume for your picture! Sailing trips on the IJsselmeer run from Volendam's harbour.

The town of **Edam** is miraculously unspoilt despite its well-known name – the famous cheese is still made here. The 17th-century town centre is dominated by the Damsluis, a vaulted and paved-over lock, and the town hall, in Louis XIV-style. Overlooking the bridge is the Kapiteinshuis (Captain's House), dating from 1540, now a museum with a 'floating cellar'. Also in Edam is a 17th-century cheese weigh house (*Kaaswaag*) displaying old cheese-making equipment and selling cheese.

From Edam it's about 12 miles (20 km) to **Hoorn**, once one of the home ports of the Dutch East Indies Company; many of its rich merchants' houses and public buildings from the Golden Age have been preserved. It was from here that several early Dutch explorers set sail, among them Abel Tasman and Willem Schouten, who, in 1616, first rounded Cape Horn (and named it Kaap Hoorn).

The road leads to another jewel – **Enkhuizen**. In the old days, great three-masted East Indiamen would lie offshore, having rounded the tip of Den Helder into the comparative calm of the Zuider Zee. Today, it's a boat and fishing harbour although cut off from direct access to the sea since 1932. The 16th-century Drommedaris, a fortified tower, is now a town cultural centre. You can climb to the top for a fine view

The way we were: Enkhuizen preserves the traditions of the old Zuider Zee.

of the IJsselmeer. The indoor section of the **Zuider Zee Museum** is located in a 1625 warehouse. Next to it (only attainable by boat and only open from April to October), is a collection of typical Zuider Zee houses, farms and workshops, illustrating life as it was between 1880 and 1932. Here you'll find a costumed cast mending nets, smoking fish and selling food. One ticket covers entry to both sections as well as the boat fare. The boat departs every 15 minutes from the railway station and from the car park.

Heading back towards Amsterdam, there's a side-trip to be made to the pretty town of **Alkmaar**. Indeed, if you're making this excursion on a Friday between mid-April and mid-September, you may well be tempted to reverse the whole order of the journey and go to Alkmaar first. The reason for this is Alkmaar's weekly cheese market, held at this time

of year in the market-place between 10 a.m. and noon.

Wholesalers converge to test the cheese and then to bid at the auction. Afterwards, the Cheese Porters, two by two, carry as many as 80 cannon-ball-shaped Edam cheeses or 12 disc-shaped Gouda cheeses on special barrows to the weigh-house. Four companies of cheese porters, all dressed in spotless white, wear straw hats

lacquered green, blue, red or yellow to denote which company they belong to.

South of Alkmaar, on the river Zaan, try to stop at yet another delightful open-air museum, **Zaanse Schans,** where wooden houses are inhabited, a grocery sells traditional sweets and a variety of windmills are still operational. In addition, there is a clock museum, an old-time bakery and a wooden shoe workshop.

ROUND THE IJSSELMEER

This trip will give you a first-hand insight into the impressive achievements of Dutch land reclamation represented by the 18 mile- (30 km) barrier dam – *Afsluitdijk* – which, in 1932, transformed the huge tidal gulf of the Zuider Zee into the freshwater lake now named the IJsselmeer, with its spacious 'polders' (stretches of reclaimed sea-bed).

After the IJtunnel leading out of Amsterdam, follow the E10 highway and the signs for Leeuwarden. You'll reach

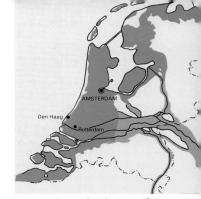

Without the 3000 km of dunes and dikes, much would be flooded by the sea (dark green) or river (light green). Windmills (below left) have been rescued and re-erected at Zaanse Schans museum. Only five are left out of a previous 700 in the area.

Middenmeer on your way north without even suspecting that you've already penetrated deep into the oldest of the reclaimed Zuider Zee polders, the Wieringermeer, completed in 1930 and put to agricultural use in 1935.

At the eastern tip of the former island of Wieringen lies the little port of Den Oever, its locks and sluices linking the IJsselmeer with the North Sea. Here begins the **Afsluitdijk**, a truly amazing feat of hydraulic engineering. In front of you, stretching as far as the eye can see, is a four-lane highway built defiantly on huge blocks of stone against the wrath of the North Sea over to your left. Four miles (7 kms) along is a café and lookout tower where the last section of the dike was put into place, albeit against tremendous water pressure that very nearly washed it away again. Explanatory plaques describe the composition and building schedule of the barrage.

Leaving the dike, you're in the province of **Friesland**, an area with its own customs and culture and even its own language, Frisian.

Just a few miles south of the dike is **Makkum**, home of one of Holland's most famous potteries for more than 300 years (see also p.101).

Nine miles (15 kms) down the coast is another village for the arts and crafts enthusiast – **Hindeloopen**. The speciality here since the 16th century has **63**

Land Below the Sea

As early as the 12th century, Dutch monasteries began reclaiming land from the sea. The technique is basically simple: lakes and estuaries are ringed with dikes, and the water is then pumped out into canals, from which it flows into rivers and out to sea. Each unit of newly reclaimed land is called a *polder*.

The job of keeping the country's feet dry is never-ending. Rising groundwater within the polder must be continuously controlled by pumping stations.

Today, 60 per cent of Holland's 15 million inhabitants live on land wrested from the sea and protected by more than 1800 miles (3000 kms) of dunes and dikes. Where jumbo jets now taxi at Schiphol Airport, a sea battle was once fought against the Spanish on the 44,500-acre (18,000-hectare) lake which then covered the area. The completed IJsselmeer polders have added nearly 5 per cent to the nation's land area.

In February 1953, an unusually violent gale, combined with an exceptional spring tide, breached the dikes in a score of places. Widespread loss of life, devastation of property and flooding of agricultural land were the tragic consequences. To prevent any recurrence of this kind of disaster, the major sea arms of the Rhine delta have been closed off in another great feat of Dutch hydraulic engineering.

been brightly coloured, hand-painted rustic furniture decorated with beautiful and intricate designs of flowers and intertwining leaves.

South now to Emmeloord and a diversion (18 miles (30 kms) each way) east to **Giethoorn**, an intriguing village with no streets – only canals – where even the milkman delivers by punt. Down the road from Emmeloord are signposts pointing right to Urk, left to Schokland. Before reclamation, both were islands jutting a few feet above the Zuider Zee. The former island of **Urk** is now a fishing village on the edge of the mainland.

A Selection of Amsterdam's Hotels and Restaurants

RECOMMENDED HOTELS

Your accommodation may have come as part of a package. If not, you have plenty of choice of places to stay in both Amsterdam and The Hague. The Netherlands Board of Tourism has a list of over 200 hotels in Amsterdam, and that's not counting boarding houses, youth and student hostels and bed-and-breakfast places in surrounding villages. Prices are quite high by international standards, but the general quality means they represent reasonable value for money, and you can be more or less certain that wherever you choose will be clean and efficiently run by pleasant, helpful people. The following selection is recommended by Berlitz and gives a range of prices and locations.

On the basis of two people sharing a double room with private bath and including breakfast, the price guide below applies (see p. 112 for a note on single rooms). You may find that reductions apply in off-season winter months, but at popular times you should reserve all lower-priced rooms to avoid disappointment.

  ❚ below f200   ❚❚ f200–400   ❚❚❚ over f400

CENTRAL AMSTERDAM

American   ❚❚❚
Leidsekade 97
1017 PN Amsterdam
Tel. 624 53 22
Fax 625 32 36
186 rooms. Architectural land mark. Includes popular, outdoor restaurant.

Amstel Intercontinental   ❚❚❚
Professor Tulpplein 1
1018 GX Amsterdam
Tel. 622 60 60
Fax 622 58 08
79 rooms. Palatial 19th-century building overlooking the River Amstel, renovated to pristine splendour and luxury. Indoor pool. Riverside restaurant, La Rive.

Ascot ▯▯▯
Damrak 95–98
1012 LP Amsterdam
Tel. 626 00 66
Fax 627 09 82
Centrally located near Dam Square. Modern canal-house style building. Good views from some rooms.

Asterisk ▯
Den Texstraat 16
1017 ZA Amsterdam
Tel. 626 23 96
Fax 638 27 90
19 rooms. modest surroundings. Near Rijksmuseum. No restaurant.

Barbizon Palace ▯▯▯
Golden Tulip
Prins Hendrikkade 59-72
1012 AD Amsterdam
Tel. 556 45 64
Fax 624 33 53
268 rooms in restored old and new buildings near Centraal Station. Health club. Bizonder (extraordinary) 'brown café' with outdoor terrace, and Vermeer Restaurant.

Belga ▯
Hartenstraat 8
1016 CB Amsterdam
Tel. 624 90 80
Fax 623 68 62
10 rooms. Small, family hotel, situated in pleasant area behind the Dam Palace.

Doelen Karena ▯▯
Nieuwe Doelenstraat 24
1012 CP Amsterdam
Tel. 622 07 22
Fax 622 10 84
45 rooms, near Muntplein. One of the oldest hotels in Amsterdam and reputedly where Rembrandt painted *The Night Watch*.

Fantasia ▯
Nieuwe Keizersgracht 16
1018 DR Amsterdam
Tel. 623 82 59; fax 622 39 13
19 rooms. Good value hotel, situated near the Royal Carré Theater.

Grand Amsterdam ▯▯▯
Oudezijds Voorburgwal 197
1012 EX Amsterdam
Tel. 555 31 11/555 32 22
In old part of city near Dam Square, situated around beautiful quiet courtyard. 160 rooms, converted from former City Hall. Excellent restaurant.

Van Haalen ▯
Prinsengracht 520
1017 KJ Amsterdam
Tel. 626 43 34
20 rooms in canalside houses. Central, near Leidseplein.

Het Canal House ▯▯
Keizersgracht 148
1015 CX Amsterdam
Tel. 622 51 82; fax 624 13 17 **67**

26 rooms in fine 17th-century house overlooking the Keizersgracht canal.

Hotel Ibis
Amsterdam Centre
Stationsplein 49
1012 AB Amsterdam
Tel. 638 99 99
Reservations 638 30 80
Fax 620 01 56
177 rooms. Modern restaurant and hotel, next to Centraal Station.

Marriott
Stadhouderskade 21
1054 ES Amsterdam
Tel. 607 55 55
Fax 607 55 11
395 rooms. Modern and central, popular with tour groups. Excellent Port O'Amsterdam Restaurant.

Die Port van Cleve
Nieuwezijds Voorburgwal 178
1012 SJ Amsterdam
Tel. 624 48 60
Fax 622 02 40
120 rooms. Conveniently located near Centraal Station. Fine restaurant with tiled frieze.

Pulitzer
Prinsengracht 315-331
1016 GZ Amsterdam
Tel. 523 52 35
Fax 627 67 53

246 rooms. Excellent restaurant in 24 beautiful canalside houses.

Ramada Renaissance
Kattengat 1
1012 SZ Amsterdam
Tel. 621 22 23
Fax 627 52 45
425 rooms (formerly the Sonesta Hotel) in old and new buildings near Centraal Station. Comfortable, old-fashioned luxury.

Rembrandt Karena
Herengracht 255
1016 BJ Amsterdam
Tel. 622 17 27
Fax 625 06 30
111 rooms, facing the canal and near the Royal Palace.

Scandic Crown
Victoria
Damrak 1
1012 LG Amsterdam
Tel. 623 42 55
Fax 625 29 97
One of Amsterdam's best hotels. 300 rooms, near Centraal Station. Indoor pool. Seasons Restaurant.

Vondel
Vondelstraat 24-30
1054 GE Amsterdam
Tel. 612 01 20
Fax 685 43 21
38 rooms. Near Vondelpark and Museumplein. No restaurant.

SOUTH AND WEST AMSTERDAM

Apollofirst ▯▯

Apollolaan 123
1077 AP Amsterdam
Tel. 673 03 33
Fax 675 03 48
35 rooms. Friendly atmosphere, south of Vondelpark. Good French restaurant.

Cok First Class Hotel ▯▯

Koninginneweg 34
1075 CZ Amsterdam
Tel. 664 61 11
Fax 664 53 04
40 rooms. Near Museumplein and Vondelpark. No restaurant.

Forte Crest Apollo ▯▯▯

Apollolaan 2
1077 BA Amsterdam
Tel. 673 59 22
Fax 570 57 44
217 rooms. Terrace with view of canals.

Garden Hotel ▯▯▯

Dijsselhofplantsoen 7
1077 BJ Amsterdam
Tel 664 21 21
Fax 679 93 56
98 rooms. This hotel has all modern comforts, and the De Kersentuin Restaurant is definitely worth a visit.

Hilton ▯▯▯

Apollolaan 138
1077 BG Amsterdam
Tel. 678 07 80
Fax 662 66 88
261 rooms. The height of comfort and luxury. Kei (Japanese) and terrace restaurants.

Holiday Inn ▯▯▯

De Boelelaan 2
1083 HJ Amsterdam
Tel. 646 23 00
Fax 646 47 90
261 rooms in modern block. All modern comforts.

Novotel Amsterdam ▯▯

Europaboulevard 10
1083 AD Amsterdam
Tel. 541 11 23
Fax 646 28 23
598 rooms in modern block near the exhibition centre.

Okura ▯▯▯

Ferdinand Bolstraat 333
1072 LH Amsterdam
Tel. 678 71 11
Fax 671 23 44
Large, modern block, 370 rooms. Spectacular view from the Ciel Bleu Restaurant up on the 23rd floor. Yamazato (Japanese) Restaurant.

69

Sander ‖
Jacob Obrechtstraat 69
1071 KJ Amsterdam
Tel. 662 75 74
Fax 679 60 67
Pleasant, modest hotel. 20 rooms. Near Concertgebouw. Bar and light snacks available. Open 24 hours.

THE HAGUE (DEN HAAG)

Bel Air ‖
Johan de Wittlaan 30
2517 JR Den Haag
Tel. (070) 351 20 21
Fax (070) 351 26 82
350 rooms in modern block near Congress Centre. Indoor swimming pool.

Corona ‖
Buitenhof 39-42
2513 AH Den Haag
Tel. (070) 363 79 30
Fax (070) 361 57 85
26 rooms. Very handy central location near Parliament. Good restaurant and brasserie.

Des Indes
Intercontinental ‖‖‖
Lange Voorhout 54
2514 EG Den Haag

Tel. (07 0) 363 29 32
Fax (070) 345 17 21
76 rooms in elegant building overlooking tree-lined central square.

Paleis Hotel ‖
Molenstraat 26
2513 BL Den Haag
Tel. (070) 362 46 21
Fax (070) 361 45 33
20 rooms. Centrally located. No restaurant.

Parkhotel Den Haag ‖‖
Molenstraat 53
2513 BJ Den Haag
Tel. (070) 362 43 71
Fax (070) 361 45 25
114 rooms. Centrally located. No restaurant.

Promenade ‖‖
Van Stolkweg 1
2585 JL Den Haag
Tel. (070) 352 51 61
Fax (070) 354 10 46
100 rooms. Modern block on the edge of a park. Fine collection of modern paintings and two very good restaurants.

Sofitel ‖‖
Koningin Julianaplein 35
2595 AA Den Haag
Tel. (070) 381 49 01
Fax (070) 382 59 27
143 rooms. Modern block above Centraal Station.

SCHEVENINGEN

Badhotel

Gevers Deijnootweg 15
2586 BB Scheveningen
Tel. (070) 351 22 21
Fax (070) 355 58 70
90 rooms. A delightful hotel (take no notice of the name!) near the sea and the town centre.

Carlton Beach Hotel

Gevers Deijnootweg 201
2586 HZ Scheveningen
Tel. (070) 354 14 14
Fax (070) 352 00 20
183 rooms, next to beach. Outdoor dining. Two restaurants. Indoor pool and health club.

Europa Hotel

Zwolsestraat 2
2587 VJ Scheveningen
Tel. (070) 351 26 51
Fax (070) 350 64 73
174 rooms close to sea. Indoor swimming pool, sauna, fitness centre, conference rooms. Two restaurants.

Steigenburger Kurhaus

Gevers Deijnootplein 30
2586 CK Scheveningen
Tel. 070) 352 00 52
Fax (070) 416 26 46
Splendidly monumental spa-hotel

with 241 rooms on seafront. Swimming pools, health club. It boasts a buffet as well as the well-known and magnificent Kandinsky Restaurant.

SCHIPHOL AIRPORT

Barbizon Schiphol Golden Tulip

Kruisweg 495
2132 NA Hoofddorp
Tel. (020) 655 05 50
Fax (020) 653 49 99
244 rooms. All modern comforts and the De Meerlanden Restaurant.

Hilton International Schiphol

Herbergierstraat 1
1118 ZK Amsterdam
Tel. (020) 603 45 67
Fax (020) 604 14 67
262 rooms. All modern comforts. Indoor swimming pool.

Ibis Amsterdam Airport

Schipholweg 181
1171 PK Amsterdam
Tel. (020) 502 51 00
Fax (020) 657 01 99
508 rooms in large, modern block. **71**

RECOMMENDED RESTAURANTS

With several hundred restaurants in Amsterdam to choose from, where do you start? To give you some guidance, we have made a selection covering a range of locations, types of cuisine and prices. However, the face of Amsterdam restaurant land is always changing, so no list can be completely up-to-date. Take local advice when you can.

There are few really low-cost eating places, although you'll find some bargains pizza and pasta joints, and the 'tourist menu' (see p. 104) is usually an economical option. Look out also for set menus, offered by most restaurants (including some of the best) – they usually represent good value. Unfortunately, unlike some big cities, you cannot assume that 'ethnic' restaurants will always be cheaper than others.

As a basic guide, we have used the following symbols to give an idea of the price for a three-course meal, for one, including service and tax, but without wine. (Keep in mind that drinks, especially wine, will increase bills considerably.)

| | below £50 | | | £50–80 | | | | above £80 |

CENTRAL AMSTERDAM

Albatros ||
Westerstraat 264
1015 MT Amsterdam
Tel. 627 99 32; fax 622 26 17
Inventive seafood specialities in cosy, family-run restaurant. Dinner only. Closed Sunday.

De Blauwe Hollander |
Leidsekruisstraat 28
1017 RJ Amdsterdam
Tel. 623 30 14
Dinner only. Dutch specialities in generous portions.

Bols Taverne ||
Rozengracht 106
1016 NH Amdsterdam
Tel. 624 57 52

Quiet, elegant fish restaurant in a converted warehouse. Closed Saturday lunchtime and Sunday.

La Cacerola

Weteringstraat 41
1017 SM Amsterdam
Tel. 626 53 97
Spanish cuisine. Dinner only. Closed Sunday.

La Camargue

Reguliersdwarsstraat 7
1017 BJ Amsterdam
Tel. 623 93 52
Elegant surroundings. Mediterranean cooking.

Da Canova

Warmoesstraat 9
1012 HT Amsterdam
Tel. 626 67 25
Italian cuisine. Dinner only. Closed Sunday and Monday.

Christophe

Leliegracht 46
1015 DH Amsterdam
Tel. 625 08 07; fax 638 91 32
Behind the Westerkerk. Southern French and Mediterranean cuisine, Michelin star and an amazing interior. Dinner only. Closed Sunday.

Dynasty

Reguliersdwarsstraat 30
1017 BM Amsterdam
Tel. 626 84 00

Chinese, Vietnamese, South-East Asian and Thai cuisine. Delightful surroundings and outdoor dining in summer. Dinner only. Closed Tuesday.

La Forge

Korte Leidsedwarstraat 26
1017 RC Amsterdam
Tel. 624 00 95
French-style bistro. Intimate, romantic atmosphere with excellent value cuisine. Open until midnight.

Green Cuisine

Beulingstraat 9
1017 BA Amsterdam
Tel. 627 57 55
Vegetarian in the main, with some fish dishes. Charming, informal surroundings.

De Groene Lanteerne

Haarlemmerstraat 43
1013 EJ Amsterdam
Tel. 624 19 52
Traditional Dutch interior and cooking in the unusual setting of a 300-year-old room. Closed Sunday and Monday.

t'Heertje

Herenstraat 16
1015 CA Amsterdam
Tel. 625 81 27
Dutch cooking, bistro-style. Closed Wednesday.

73

Holland's Glorie

Kerkstraat 222
1017 GV Amsterdam
Tel. 624 47 64
Dutch and international cuisine. Dinner only.

De Impressionist

Keizersgracht 312
1016 EX Amsterdam
Tel. 627 66 66
Pleasant, light basement with first-class French cuisine using inventive, fresh ingredients. Good value set menus. Dinner only. Closed Sunday.

Kopenhagen

Rokin 84
1012 KX Amsterdam
Tel. 624 93 76
Danish specialities. Closed Sunday.

Koriander

Amstel 212
1017 AH Amsterdam
Tel. 627 78 79
Brasserie. Open till midnight. Dinner only. Closed Sunday and Monday.

Lana-Thai

Warmoesstraat 10
1012 JD Amsterdam
Tel. 624 21 79; fax 420 01 20
Thai cuisine. Traditional ambience.

Land van Walem

Keizersgracht 449
1017 DK Amsterdam
Tel. 625 35 44
Informal, nouveau-chic brasserie and café. French and Dutch menus, newspapers and magazines provided! Lunch and dinner.

Lido Brasserie

Leidsekade 105
1017 MB Amsterdam
Tel. 626 21 06
Informal dining in casino complex, (which also houses the French/Asian Gauguin Restaurant and a waterside café).

Lucius

Spuistraat 247
1012 VP Amsterdam
Tel. 624 18 31
Fish and shellfish specialities. Traditional but informal. Dinner only.

Manchurian

Leidseplein 10a
1017 PW Amsterdam
Tel. 623 13 30
Oriental cuisine. Very good food in a lively part of town.

De Oesterbar

Leidseplein 10
1017 PT Amsterdam
Tel. 623 29 88
Famous for its oysters and situated alongside the lively Leidseplein.

O'Henry's ▯
Rokin 89
1012 KL Amsterdam
Tel. 625 14 98
English pub with appropriate food
and also some international dishes. Open to 1 a.m., to 2 a.m. Friday and Saturday.

Paddy's Inn ▯
Herenstraat 14
1015 CA Amsterdam
Tel. 624 22 29
Irish food and steaks. Informal at-
mosphere. Dinner only.

Pancake Corner ▯
Kleine Gartmanplantsoen 51
1017 RP Amsterdam
Tel. 627 63 03
Pancakes of all kinds, mussels a
speciality.

Le Pêcheur ▯▯
Reguliersdwarsstraat 32
1017 BM Amsterdam
Tel. 624 31 21
Seafood specialities in the midst
of a very lively part of Amsterdam. Outside eating in a small
garden in summer. Open till midnight. Closed lunchtime Saturday
and Sunday.

Pied de Cochon ▯▯
Noorderstraat 19
1017 TR Amsterdam
Tel. 623 76 77

Bistro-style French country cooking. Dinner only.

Les Quatre Canetons ▯▯▯
Prinsengracht 1111
1017 JJ Amsterdam
Tel. 624 63 07
First-class French cuisine in one
of The Netherlands' top restau-
rants. Expensive but worthwhile.
Closed Sunday.

't Seepared ▯▯
1st floor
Rembrandtsplein 22
1017 CV Amsterdam
Tel. 622 17 59
Seafood specialities. Outdoor
dining as well. Open till midnight.

Sichuan Food ▯▯
Reguliersdwarsstraat 35
1017 BK Amsterdam
Tel. 626 93 27
Chinese cuisine, delicious spicy
Szechuan specialities. Dinner
only. Closed Wednesday.

De Silveren Spiegel ▯▯
Kattengat 4
1012 SZ Amsterdam
Tel. 624 65 89
Fresh local products inventively
prepared. Sample them relaxing in
the surroundings of two charming
old houses. Closed Saturday
lunchtime and Sunday. **75**

Sjef Schets ‖

Leidsestraat 20
1017 PA Amsterdam
Tel. 622 80 85
Outdoor Dutch dining. Closed
Saturday lunchtime and Sunday.

Sluizer ‖

Utrechtsestraat 41-45
1017 VH Amsterdam
Tel. 626 35 57
Two restaurants, one specializing
in fish, the other in French cuisine.
Lively, easy-going atmosphere.

Speciaal ‖

Nieuwe Leliestraat 142
1015 SX Amsterdam
Tel. 624 97 06
Indonesian cuisine in the heart of
fashionable Jordaan. Pleasant,
quiet restaurant.

't Swarte Schaep ‖‖‖

1st floor
Korte Leidsedwarsstraat 24
1017 RC Amsterdam
Tel. 622 30 21
17th-century interior decor.
French/international menu.

Tom Yam ‖

Staalstraat 23
1011 JM Amsterdam
Tel. 622 95 33
Inventive Thai cuisine. Popular
with the artistic crowd. The Tom
Ka Kay soup is a must.

Treasure ‖

Nieuwezijds Voorburgwal 115
1012 RH Amsterdam
Tel. 626 09 15
Chinese cuisine – probably the
best in Amsterdam. Ambitious
multi-course menus available.

Les Trois Neufs ‖

Prinsengracht 999
1017 KM Amsterdam
Tel. 622 90 44
French classic cuisine. Good
value. Closed Monday.

SOUTH AND WEST AMSTERDAM

Beddington's ‖‖‖

Roelof Hartstraat 6–8
1071 VH Amsterdam
Tel. 676 52 01
Fresh, inventive international
cooking in elegant, modern surroundings. High prices. Closed
Sunday.

Bojo ‖

Lange Leidedwarsstraat 51
1017 NG Amsterdam
Tel. 622 74 34
Best value Indonesian restaurant
in town. Expect to have to wait for
a table – stays open until 6 a.m.

Brasserie Van Baerle ‖

Van Baerlestraat 158
1071 BG Amsterdam
Tel. 679 15 32

Pleasant, friendly restaurant with outdoor seating. Booking advisable. Closed Saturday.

Cajun ‖

Ceintuurbaan 260
1072 GH Amsterdam
Tel. 664 47 29

Louisiana 'cajun' food. Blackened (spicy, fast-grilled) specialities.

Les Frères ‖

Bosboom Toussainstraat 70
1054 AV Amsterdam
Tel. 618 79 05

French, bistro-style. Dinner only. Closed Sunday.

La Grande Bouffe ‖

1e Constantijn Huygensstraat 115
1054 BV Amsterdam
Tel. 618 81 91

Classic French, Dinner only, Closed Saturday.

Halvemaan ‖‖‖

Van Leyenberghlaan 20
1082 GM Amsterdam
Tel. 644 03 48

Creative cooking, with influences from Italy, France and the Orient. Waterside seating in summer. Closed Sunday.

Hamilcar ‖

Overtoom 306
1054 JC Amsterdam
Tel. 683 79 81

Tunisian cuisine. Dinner only. Closed Monday.

Het Bosch ‖‖‖

Jollenpad 10
1081 KC Amsterdam
Tel. 644 58 00

View. Outdoor dining. Pleasant lakeside terrace. Closed Sunday October-March.

De Kersentuin ‖‖‖

Garden Hotel
Dijsselhofplantsoen 7
1077 BJ Amsterdam
Tel. 664 21 21

Exclusive French/international cuisine, undoubtedly one of the most elegant restaurants in town. The name means 'cherry orchard'. Art exhibitions are held in the lounge. Booking essential. Closed Sunday.

Keyzer Bodega ‖

Van Baerlestraat 96
1071 BB Amsterdam
Tel. 671 14 41

Dutch and international cuisine next door to Concertgebouw. Charming interior with ferns and wood-carved panels. Booking advisable. Dress accordingly. Closed Sunday.

77

In den Nedehoven ‖
Nederhoven 13
1083 AM Amsterdam
Tel. 642 56 19
French cuisine. Outdoor dining. Closed Saturday and Sunday lunchtime.

Orient ‖
Van Baerlestraat 21
1071 AN Amsterdam
Tel. 673 49 58
Indonesian cuisine. Closed Saturday and Sunday lunchtime.

Parkrestaurant ‖‖
Rosarium
Europaboulevard
Amstelpark 1
1083 HZ Amsterdam
Tel. 644 40 85
International cuisine. Outdoor dining. Closed Sunday.

Ravel ‖
Gelderlandplein 2
1082 LA Amsterdam
Tel. 644 16 43
Charming taverna. Closed Sunday lunchtime.

Trechter (de Wit) ‖‖
Hobbemakade 63
1071 XL Amsterdam
Tel. 671 12 63
Innovative French cuisine. Book in advance. Dinner only. Closed **78** Sunday and Monday.

OUTSIDE AMSTERDAM

Aviorama ‖
3rd floor
Schipholweg 1
1118 AA Amsterdam
Tel. (020) 604 11 05
International cuisine at Schiphol Airport. Good views and handy for when you've missed your flight home.

Gekroonde Hamer ‖
Breestraat 24
2011 ZZ Haarlem
Tel. (023) 312243
Dinner only. Outdoor dining. Closed Sunday.

Het Kampje ‖
Kerkstraat 56
1191 JE Ouderkerk aan de Amstel
Tel. (02963) 1943
Outdoor traditional dining. Closed on Wednesday, Saturday and Sunday.

Hilda ‖
Wagenweg 214
2012 NM Haarlem
Tel. (023) 312871
Very good and reasonable Indonesian cuisine. Dinner only. Closed Saturday and Sunday lunchtime and all day Monday.

Klein Paardenburg ▮▮▮
Amstelzijde 59
1184 TZ Ouderkerk aan de
Amstel
Tel. (02963) 1335
Notably good cuisine. Outdoor
dining. Closed Saturday lunch-
time, Sunday and Monday.

De Meerpaal ▮▮
Noordeinde 78a
1121 AG Amsterdam
Tel. (02908) 3381
In Landsmeer. Closed Saturday
and Sunday lunchtime.

Molen De Dikkert ▮▮▮
Amsterdamseweg 104a
1182 HG Amstelveen
Tel. (020) 641 13 78
Notably good Dutch cuisine.
Pleasant elegant restaurant in con-
verted 17th-century mill. Closed
Saturday lunchtime and Sunday.

Paardenburg ▮▮▮
Amstelzijde 55
1184 TZ Ouderkerk aan de
Amstel
Tel. (02963) 1210
19th-century murals. Delightful
waterside terrace. Closed Sunday.

Rôtisserie ▮▮▮
Ile de France
Pieter Lastmanweg 9
1181 XG Amstelveen
Tel. (020) 645 35 09

Good French cuisine. Closed Saturday lunchtime, Sunday and
Monday.

THE HAGUE (DEN HAAG)

Le Gobelet ▮▮
Noordeinde 143
2514 GG Den Haag
Tel. (070) 346 58 38
Delightful French bistro. Open till
midnight. Closed Sunday.

La Grande Bouffe ▮▮
Maziestraat 10
2514 GT Den Haag
Tel. (070) 365 42 74
French haute cuisine. Closed Sat-
urday and Sunday lunchtime and
Monday.

Jean Martin ▮▮
Groenewegje 115
2515 LP Den Haag
Tel. (070) 380 28 95
French cuisine. Dinner only.
Closed Sunday and Monday.

Julien ▮▮
Vos in Tuinstraat 2a
2514 BX Den Haag
Tel. (070) 365 86 02
Open till midnight. Closed Satur-
day and Sunday lunchtime. **79**

Radèn Ajoe IIII
Lange Poten 31
2511 CM Den Haag
Tel. (070) 364 45 92
Indonesian cuisine. Closed Sunday lunchtime.

Da Roberto IIII
Noordeinde 196
2514 GS Den Haag
Tel. (070) 346 49 77
Italian cuisine. Closed Saturday and Sunday lunchtime.

Roma II
Papestraat 22
2513 AW Den Haag
Tel. (070) 346 23 45
Italian cuisine. Closed Sunday lunchtime and Tuesday.

Royal Dynasty II
Noordeinde 123
2514 GG Den Haag
Tel. (070) 365 25 98
Thai cuisine. Closed Monday.

Saur IIII
Lange Voorhout 51
2514 EC Den Haag
Tel. (070) 346 33 44
Notably good seafood. Closed Saturday lunchtime and Sunday.

Table du Roi II
Prinsestraat 130
2513 CH Den Haag
Tel. (070) 346 19 08

Dinner only. Closed Monday and Tuesday.

De Verliefde Kreeft I
Bleijenburg 11
2511 VC Den Haag
Tel. (070) 364 45 22
Seafood. Closed Saturday and Sunday lunchtime.

SCHEVENINGEN

Le Bon Mangeur I
Wassenaarsestraat 119
2586 AM Scheveningen
Tel. (070) 355 92 13
French, bistro-style. Dinner only. Closed Sunday and Monday.

Ducdolf I
Dr Lelykade 5
2583 CL Scheveningen
Tel. (070) 355 76 92
Seafood specialities.

La Galleria I
Gevers Deijnootplein 120
2586 CP Scheveningen
Tel. (070) 352 11 76
Italian cuisine. Outdoor dining.

Radèn Mas IIII
Gevers Deijnootplein 125
2586 CX Scheveningen
Tel. (070) 354 54 32
Good value Indonesian cuisine.

The busy fleet gets out into the North Sea via the sluice gates at Den Oever.

From Emmeloord, the main road south west is signposted to Lelystad and Amsterdam. Already you're on land reclaimed after the Afsluitdijk was finally closed. This is the 120,000-acre (48,560 hectare) Noordoost (North-East) polder, completed in 1942 and the oldest of the three you will now drive across. It all looks well-developed here, yet only a few decades ago this land formed the bottom of the sea.

As you drive towards Amsterdam, notice the different stages of polder develop-

Over the centuries, huge tracts of fertile land have been created from marshes, lakes and the sea itself.

ment. The Oostelijk (East) Flevoland, completed in 1957 – is already widely cultivated – and the contiguous Zuidelijk (South) Flevoland, drained in 1968, looks emptier and newer with its Lego-like farms. Between Lelystad and Almere lies an uncultivated marshy area, the Oostvaardersplassen – a paradise for birds.

Shortly after Almere, a bridge connects Flevoland to the mainland. Beyond stands the forbidding **Castle of Muiden** (*Muiderslot*), first built in the 13th century. One of only two unaltered medieval castles in Holland, it now houses a historical museum.

HAARLEM AND THE TULIP TRAIL
Pop. 150,000
Amsterdam 12 miles (19km)
A treasure house of historical buildings, Haarlem's central square (*Groote Markt*) is dominated by the massive **St.-Bavokerk**. Inside this 15th-century monument is one of the finest church organs in Europe, with its 5000 pipes,

installed in 1738. Both Mozart and Handel played on it, and you can hear the quality for yourself during recitals on Thursdays at 3 p.m. from mid-May to August.

The **Vleeshal** (meat market) is one of Holland's finest Renaissance buildings. Just off the square, the **Frans Hals Museum** is devoted to the town's most famous son. Eleven of his paintings are on display within, and the house itself is a gem, dating from 1608 and with a beautifully preserved 17th-century garden. Hals lived in the house in his later years.

At the height of summer you might like to continue on to **Zandvoort** for a dip in the bracing North Sea. In August, banners herald the grand prix car race, while at any time of the year you can try your luck in the town's casino.

From mid-April to the end of May the floral route to the south of Haarlem beckons. Never in your life will you have seen so many tulips and other cultivated flowers as in the thousands of hectares south through Hillegom to Lisse, all planted in flawless colour-co-ordinated rectangles. Just before Lisse is the 69 acre (28 hectare) **Keukenhof**, a showpiece flower garden which, for two months from the end of March to the end of May blazes with crocus, hyacinth, narcissus, tulip and azalea displays. Dotted around the gardens are spectacular greenhouses, shops, a windmill and a restaurant.

From Lisse it's a short drive to the huge **flower auction hall** (*Bloemenveiling*) at **Legmeerdijk**. Here, in one vast building, nine million cut flowers and three quarters of a million pot-plants are sold every *day*. Visitors are admitted (Monday to Friday from 7.30-11 a.m.) to a mile (1.6 km) long raised walkway above the floor. There is a short cut for those who don't want to make the whole circuit.

*E*very spring, Dutch flower-growers come together to show off their products at the gardens at Keukenhof, south of Haarlem.

Stop to watch the auction rooms in action. The famous electronic clock starts at a higher price than anyone is going to pay and winds very rapidly down. Simultaneously, attendants wheel trains of flowers or plants through the auction room for the buyers to see. When the clock falls to a price they wish to bid at, the bidders push a button to stop it and state how many lots they want at that price. The clock then instantly flashes up to its high starting figure and the whole process begins again. It all happens much faster than it takes to describe! Meanwhile, as one procession of trucks arrives outside with more millions of flowers, another loads up and drives off with those that have just been sold.

LEIDEN

Pop. 110,000
Amsterdam 25 miles (40km)
This old university town, birthplace of Rembrandt and Jan Steen, can be conveniently visited as an extension to a trip to Haarlem and the bulb country or as a stop on the way to The Hague, Delft or Rotterdam.

The tourist information office at Stationsplein 210, opposite the railway station, is a good place to start from. You might like to visit the tall windmill, **De Valk**, only a few hundred metres away. It dates from 1743 and contains a fine collection of miller's equipment. If the wind is suitable, the mill is put into operation. (Closed on Mondays.)

The **Lakenhal**, on Oude Singel, former guildhall of the town's clothmakers, was built in 1639. It now houses the city museum's historical and decorative-arts collection, as well as oils by the Renaissance painter Lucas van Leyden.

The nearby **Rijksmuseum voor Volkenkunde** (Ethnographic Museum) is rich in exhibits from outside Europe. At the back of the museum's garden stands at 17th-century town gate, the Morspoort, and near it a rebuilt windmill.

Breestraat is the busy main street of the **old town**. Up here, on the left-hand side, is the

B ands of rainbow colours bring visitors flocking each spring to the Dutch bulbfields.

splendid Renaissance façade of the Stadhuis (town hall), the only part of the original building to survive a disastrous fire in 1929. The first turning left after this will bring you to Stadhuisplein, the marketplace and a **covered bridge**, built in 1642 (though the neo-classical arcades date from 1825).

Beyond the bridge lies the heart of the old town with the artificial fortified hillock, the **Burcht**, dating from the 12th century. Some of the town's oldest almshouses, and the 14th-century Hooglandse Kerk grace this area.

The massive, Gothic **St.-Pieterskerk** stands out to the west of Breestraat. It was consecrated in 1121, though not completed until the early 15th century. Here John Robinson, whose preaching inspired the Pilgrim Fathers, lies buried. One of the outer walls bears a plaque in his memory, put there by American admirers in the 19th century.

In Kloksteeg, opposite this plaque, is the **Jan Pesijnhofje**, another of those attractive clusters of almshouses for which Leiden is famous. This one was founded in 1683 by an ancestor of President Franklin D. Roosevelt.

Kloksteeg leads down to the pretty **Rapenburg Canal,** across which is the **Academie**, the main building of the University. Founded in 1575 by William the Silent as a reward for the town's valiant resis- **85** tance to a protracted Spanish siege, the Academie still looks virtually the same as it did 400 years ago. The flourishing Botanical Garden behind it dates from the same period.

Turn right at the bottom of Kloksteeg and follow the Rapenburg Canal. Here, at No. 28, the **Rijksmuseum voor Oudheden** (National Antiquities Museum) houses The Netherland's finest collection of Egyptian mummies and hieroglyphic inscriptions.

THE HAGUE

Pop. 460,000
Amsterdam 35 miles (57 km)
Den Haag, or The Hague, is Holland's diplomatic city and seat of government, as well as the home of the International Court of Justice. Although Amsterdam is the capital city, The Hague can claim equal status as home of the law and Parliament.

Undoubtedly, the jewel of The Hague is the **Binnenhof**, now the seat of Parliament. Monumental gateways provide access to a rectangular courtyard lined with government buildings. The magnificent medieval **Ridderzaal**, or Knight's Hall, which dates back to the 13th century, stands at the heart of it all. Supported by great beams and adorned by stained-glass windows, it emanates a sense of victory. It is here that the Queen arrives each September in her golden coach to open Parliament. Guided tours available year-round from Monday to Saturday from 10 a.m. to 3.55 p.m.

For a different perspective on the old days, visit the **Gevangenpoort** (Prison Gate) **National Museum** at Buitenhof 33, with its rather gruesome exhibition of torture instruments. Guided tours take place Monday to Friday from 11 a.m. to 4 p.m. and in summer on

1. Congresgebouw
2. Haags Gemeentemuseum
3. Madurodam
4. Vredespaleis
5. Nederlands Postmuseum
6. Panorama Mesdag
7. Gevangenpoort
8. Buitenhof
9. Binnenhof
10. Mauritshuis

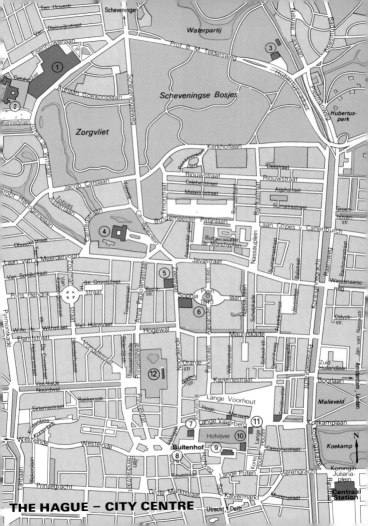

THE HAGUE – CITY CENTRE

The Hague has charming old streets as well as palaces and government buildings.

Saturdays, Sundays and public holidays from 1 p.m. to 5 p.m.

As you walk around the Hofvijver, the square pond next to the Binnenhof, you'll notice some elegant 18th-century houses on Lange Vijverberg. At one end of the pond, at Korte Vijverberg 7, the **Haags Historisch Museum**, has an interesting collection on the history of the town.

 Bordering the pond is the **Mauritshuis**, constructed by the Dutch ex-governor of northern Brazil from 1637 to 1644. It now houses one of the world's finest small art collec-

tions. Among its 400 or so paintings are several Rembrandts including *Dr Tulp's Anatomy Lesson*, Vermeer's *View of Delft* and a number of works by Jan Steen, Frans Hals and others. Open Tuesday to Saturday from 10 a.m. to 5 p.m., Sundays and public holidays from 11 a.m.

Across the Hofvijver lies the most distinguished quarter of The Hague: the rectangle formed by Kneuterdijk, Lange Vijverberg and Lange Voorhout. The **Lange Voorhout**, in particular – a broad avenue with three double rows of lime trees, lined with stately 17th- and 18th-century houses, some of which are now in use as embassies – has a particularly stylish character of its own.

Panorama Mesdag, at Zeestraat 65b, gives a detailed picture of what The Hague's seaside neighbour, Scheveningen, looked like in 1881. The vast circular painting lining the walls gives you the optical illusion of standing on a dune, enjoying a 360 degree view.

Close by, at Zeestraat 82, the **Nederlands Postmuseum** (Dutch Postal Museum) contains an exhibition of the country's stamps, history of the postal service and equipment.

From here it's a short walk to the **Vredespaleis** (Peace Palace) at Carnegieplein. Financed by the steel tycoon Andrew Carnegie in 1913, this is the seat of the International Court of Justice and related bodies. Guided tours take place from Monday to Friday at 10 and 11 a.m. and 2 and 3 p.m. The palace may be closed when the court is in session. It is best to telephone before setting out: 070-346 96 80.

On Stadhouderslaan, the **Haags Gemeentemuseum** (Municipal Museum) contains the world's largest collection of paintings by the Dutch artist Piet Mondrian, in addition to works by Picasso, Monet and van Gogh and sculptures by Henry Moore and Barbara Hepworth. Further exhibits include varied arts and crafts and a vast collection of musical instruments, both European and oriental.

The adjacent **Museon** is a modern museum covering the various facets of culture, science and technology. An advanced planetarium called the **Omniversum** (President Kennedylaan 5) has a huge domed screen able to produce a 3-D effect, augmented by a sound system that seems to surround you completely.

Children especially, but not exclusively, will love the miniature city of **Madurodam**. On its 19,000 sq yds (16,000 sq m) some 150 of Holland's most famous buildings are reproduced at $1/25$th their actual size. Moving trains and taxiing planes are there, too, along with boats loading and unloading. At dusk, 50,000 tiny lights twinkle in its streets. Madurodam even has a mayoress and a council, elected annually, of 32 local school children. It opens daily at 9 a.m. and closes at 11 p.m. (June-August), 9.30 p.m. (September), 6 p.m. (October-

89

January 6), and 10.30 p.m. (March-May).

The Queen of the Netherlands lives in **Huis ten Bosch**, an attractive palace situated in the eastern outskirts of The Hague, surrounded by delightful woodlands. Her office is in another palace, on Noordeinde, considered to be Holland's most elegant shopping street.

To round off your trip, take a walk along the sands at the famous seaside resort of **Scheveningen**, with its grand pier and the restored Kurhaus spa hotel, the proud home of Europe's largest casino.

DELFT

Pop. 88,000
Amsterdam 38 miles (61km)
About halfway between The Hague and Rotterdam, and some 15 minutes' drive from either, lies Delft, one of Holland's most picturesque towns – home of the painter Vermeer and of the distinctive blue and white pottery that bears the town's name. But tradition and conservation haven't hampered Delft's development as

an important industrial centre and home of a great technological university.

In summer, you can give your tired feet a rest by taking a tour by boat (leaving from Koornmarkt daily in summer, Sundays only during spring and autumn) on Delft's tree-lined canals spanned by graceful, high-vaulted bridges.

The canals are flanked by attractive 17th- and 18th-century houses, and the focal point of Delft is its spacious **market-place**, one of the country's most charming.

At its western end stands the gilded Renaissance **Raadhuis** (town hall), but the elongated square is dominated by the enormous **Nieuwe Kerk** (New Church). Begun in 1384, it took more than 100 years to build. This is the final resting place of William the Silent, founder of the nation (see p.14), and of many other members of the House of Orange.

Behind the town hall, the old **Boterhuis** (butter market) and **Waag** (weigh-house) can still be seen. Leave the market-place here, cross over Wijn-

The famous market-place at Delft is dominated by the towering Nieuwe Kerk.

a hired assassin in the pay of the Spanish King Philip II. The bullet holes – greatly enlarged by the probing fingers of early visitors – can still be seen near the foot of a winding staircase.

Part of the Prinsenhof is now given over to a **museum** devoted to the Dutch War of Independence (1568-1648). It also includes a number of paintings, banners and other objects pertaining to various members of the House of Orange, as well as an interesting collection of silver. Every summer, an **antique fair** is held here (the date is movable, so check first with one of the Dutch tourist offices).

Just beyond the Prinsenhof, on Oude Delft canal, is the **Museum Huis Lambert van Meerten**, which contains one of the country's most extensive collections of old Delft pottery and Dutch tiles.

haven, walk along Boterbrug – street and bridge in one – and you'll come to the Oude Delft Canal, almost 1000 years old.

The **Oude Kerk** (Old Church) 500 ft (150 m) to the right, was begun in the first part of the 13th century, and has been renovated on several occasions since. Note its heavy leaning tower with straightened turrets.

The **Prinsenhof**, nearby, formerly a convent, became the residence of William the Silent in 1572. Twelve years later, he was murdered here by

91

If it's modern Delftware that interests you, you might like to tour the town's porcelain factory, the only survivor of some 30 factories which thrived in the 17th century. On weekdays, **De Porceleyne Fles,** at Rotterdamseweg 196, welcomes visitors to view its showrooms. Another pottery, **De Delftse Pauw**, on Delftweg 133, is no less interesting.

Windmill Country

Holland's windmills, now a decorative feature of the landscape, were once essential to the country's survival. Without drainage mills, water could not have been cleared from below sea level throughout the whole of north Holland, and the countryside would still be laced with lakes.

Most of the surviving 950 windmills throughout the country are protected as monuments, and some 200 of them are still in use. Concentrations of them or unusual varieties can be seen at:

Arnhem's Open-air Museum (Openluchtmuseum), 60 miles (96km) south east of Amsterdam, where all major types of mills have been preserved.

Zaanse Schans Open-air Museum near Zaandam, 10 miles (16km) north west of Amsterdam. Several different types, including a saw mill, a paint mill and an oil mill.

Schiedam, just west of Rotterdam, where four survivors remain out of the original 18 tall stone mills which formerly dotted its ramparts.

But the most impressive line-up of windmills is to be found at **Kinderdijk**, 12 miles (20 km) east of Rotterdam. Here there are 19 mills, 17 of which turn their sails together on Saturday afternoons in July and August. At least one can be seen in operation every weekday from April to October.

Amsterdam once bristled with windmills. Today only six are left, one serving as a suburban restaurant, another overlooking the River Amstel on the southern edge of town.

What to Do

Entertainment

(Look in *Culture in Amsterdam*, *What's on in Amsterdam* and *Uit* for detailed information on entertainments, times of performances etc.)

Nightlife tends to concentrate around Leidseplein, with the vast majority of bars, restaurants and nightclubs found here. **Nightclubs** in Amsterdam are only rarely of international standard. The Lido at Max Euweplein 62 (just off Leidseplein) comes closest. Housed in a former jail, it has the city's only **casino**, with all the usual forms of gaming, roulette, blackjack etc. (There's another casino in the Kurhaus at Scheveningen.) Around Rembrandtsplein, in particular, you will encounter Holland's nearest approach to an out-and-out clip joint.

Discos are plentiful, especially around Leidseplein, but

The exciting new opera house, the Muziektheater known as 'Stopera' on Waterlooplein.

also scattered about the city and in some hotels. Entry to discos and clubs is usually free – you'll simply pay more for drinks, according to what is being offered in entertainment. It's customary to tip the cloakroom attendant and doorman.

Cinemas are concentrated around Rembrandtsplein and Leidseplein. Films are always shown in the original language with Dutch subtitles.

The internationally celebrated Royal Concertgebouw Orchestra plays in the Concertgebouw itself (*gebouw* means building) though tickets for their **concerts** can be hard to obtain. Chamber music is played in the Kleine Zaal. The Netherlands Philharmonic Orchestra performs in the Beurs van Berlage (see p.37). The Netherlands **Opera** is based at the modern Muziek-theater (at the *Stopera* on Waterlooplein).

Jazz, mostly traditional, is played at weekends in the Joseph Lam Jazzclub, van Diemenstraat 8, and evenings (except Sundays) in the Bamboo Bar, Lange Leidsedwarsstraat 64. A wider range, from traditional to progressive, may be heard at Bimhuis, Oude Schans 73–77. (Telephone the Jazzline, 626 77 64, for information on dates and times.)

Apart from visiting productions and those of local expatriate amateur groups, **theatre** is usually in Dutch, a serious barrier to most visitors.

Try to see the Dutch National **Ballet** in a classic – the *Stopera* Muziektheater is the venue – or the avant-garde Nederlands Dans Theater, much acclaimed in recent years, at the Muziektheater or the Stadsschouwburg.

The **Holland Festival** of art, music, dance and theatre takes place throughout the country, but mainly in Amsterdam, each June. Seats at star events can be difficult to obtain, unless you apply in advance. Tickets for many performances are obtainable by telephone: 621 12 11 (information and credit card bookings), or in person from the VVV at Stationsplein 10 or the Amsterdams Uitburo, Leidseplein 26 (Monday to Saturday 9 a.m. to 9 p.m.).

94

FESTIVALS IN AMSTERDAM

February-March
Just before Lent, parades, fancy dress, dancing, a larger-than-usual consumption of beer and non-stop Dutch music spills into some Amsterdam streets and bars.

March
The Amsterdam Art Weeks Festival offers a wide variety of cultural activities such as opera, dance, ballet, theatre (including English-speaking companies) and exhibitions.

April
April 30 is called Queen's Day, a public holiday when everyone turns out. Children set up stalls, selling anything from home-made cakes to broken toys. Street musicians are allowed to busk for the day and collect money. Portrait-sketchers flourish. It's unique, a local celebration you should try not to miss.

June-July
The Holland Festival is a more up-market cultural occasion of music, opera, ballet, theatre and recitals. It is paralleled by the Vondelpark Festival. From Wednesday to Sunday there are free open-air performances of music, dance and theatre, and children's plays.

August
Uitmarkt, the last weekend in August, marks the beginning of the new season. Thousands of people attend for free music and theatre performances.

September
On a Saturday at the beginning of the month, a huge floral parade makes its way from Aalsmeer to Amsterdam and back. The second Friday in the month sees the start of the Jordaan Festival, ten days of fun in this friendliest part of the old city.

November-December
In the middle of November, Holland's St. Nicolaas (or Sinterklaas) arrives by boat from Spain with his Moorish servant, Black Pete, and tours town on a white horse.

December 5, the saint's birthday, heralds *pakjesavond* (Parcels Night), a traditional family festival. The next day, Sinterklaas leaves for Spain again.

95

Sports

There's water, water every-where, so the choice of water sports is vast. In fact, so great is the demand for **boats and yachts** on the lakes near the city that it's practically impos-sible to hire a vessel at short notice during the summer.

As for the canals, you can take advantage of them by hiring **canal bikes**, (pedal-boats for two or four), **motor-boats**, or **canoes**. But these too are popular and you must book well in advance.

You can **water-ski** at some lakes and **swim** from the miles of sandy North Sea beaches, but remember that the water is at Northern European tem-peratures – so donning a wet-suit may be a good idea! (A few of the expensive hotels have indoor swimming pools.)

For **skating**, there's the Jaap Eden stadium, with both indoor and outdoor rinks, on Radioweg. The Dutch are ranked high among the world-champion speed skaters, and in winter you could watch an exciting big race here, or maybe an international ice-hockey match.

Sad to say, even in the depths of winter you are un-likely to witness throngs of skaters on the canals, whatever those old paintings may have led you to believe. Unfortu-nately, nowadays it's rarely cold enough for the waterways to freeze over.

Cruising on the River Amstel is certainly the best way to get around Amsterdam.

Off the water, **soccer** is the Dutch sporting passion. With the right contacts you could get a ticket to see Amsterdam's idolized Ajax (pronounced EYE-AX) in action.

Cycling is a favourite means of getting about in both town and country. For a pleasure ride, pick a Sunday if you can, when the traffic is light. The flatness of the land is a distinct advantage – if the wind isn't against you.

Walking in the city is made even more interesting if you pick up route leaflets from the VVV, and the villages to the north are close enough together to walk from one to another. Alternatively take a hike along the sandy beaches of the North Sea coast for a change from city streets.

There are more than 30 **tennis** courts for hire at the Tennis-centrum Nieuw BV at Lotsylaan 8 (bus 26 from Leidseplein or tram 5). For other tennis, and also **squash** facilities, contact the VVV tourist information office, tel. 626 64 44.

For **horse-riding**, try the Amsterdamse Bos (Amsterdam Woods). The stables here will hire out horses for group rides.

Golfers are less well catered for due to scarcity of land. Unless you can contrive an introduction to the Amsterdam Golf Club at Duivendrecht or the Olympus Golf Club near Amstelveen, you may be reduced to doing a circuit of **mini-golf** in Sloterpark (President Allendelaan, west of the city centre).

Shopping

Modern patterns of retailing have had less impact in Amsterdam than in most capital cities. There are no famous or exclusive shopping streets, no vast 'malls' or megastores.

Instead, hundreds of small shops have survived, scattered throughout the compact central area, and offering everything from the basic essentials to antique Delftware. The atmosphere resembles that of an extended village or an old **97** market town. That's the way the locals like it, and visitors agree. Generally Nieuwendijk and Kalverstraat are good for clothes and department stores as well as Leidsestraat and Rokin, although they are more expensive. The new Magna Plaza centre behind the Palace offers a collection of specialized shops in the former 19th century post office.

Shopping Hours

Most shops are open from 10 a.m. to 6 p.m., Monday to Saturday (though many don't open on Mondays till 1 p.m.). Some stay open until 9 p.m. on Thursdays.

What to Buy

If you're looking for something specifically Dutch, there are plenty of quality products to choose from. You won't find any cheap bargains but you'll be assured of value for money.

Flowers and **plants** are of exceptional quality and variety – if you can transport them and there are no import restrictions

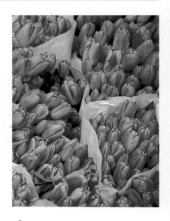

Living jewels: millions of flowers are sold every day.

imposed by the country you are entering. Traders can mail bulbs and plants.

Dutch cigars are world-famous and reasonably priced. If you are buying them as a present, find out the recipient's preference in advance – there's such a wide range available.

Dutch gin (*jenever*), made with juniper berries, is more fruity than fiery.

Diamonds are Forever

Or are they? If you buy diamonds as an investment, dealers will urge you not to wear them in order to avoid damage. Whether you are a potential customer or not, you are welcome to tour any of a dozen diamond-cutting and polishing centres in Amsterdam. Notices all over town invite you to visit diamond exhibitions and workshops (there's no obligation to buy, of course). Taxi drivers are also well primed to whisk you to their favourite diamond merchant if they hear a mention of the word.

Amsterdam has a 400-year reputation to uphold – an Amsterdam cutter was given the nerve-racking responsibility of turning the biggest rough diamond ever found, the Cullinan, into polished gemstones. The city's importance declined after the Nazis persecuted and killed many Jewish artisans and dealers but efforts have been made to wrest back its leading role.

The Four 'C's: Carat, Colour, Clarity and Cut

A diamond's weight is measured in carats and points. 100 points = 1 carat = 0.2 grams. Because of the rarity of larger stones, they make more money per carat, so the bigger the better. How much for a flawless one carat stone? As the tycoon said of his yacht, if you need to ask, you can't afford it, but the answer is about f35,000.

Blue-white (virtually colourless) is the standard 'colour' – tinges of yellow reduce the value. Clear strong colours (pink, blue, green or a full yellow) are rare and can be very valuable.

Experts are needed in all matters relating to diamonds, but perhaps most of all to judge clarity. From 'flawless' to 'VVSI' (very very small inclusions) to 'VSI' to 'SI' and 'piqué', their decision makes all the difference.

The word 'cut' is misleading. After the initial cutting to size, a diamond's many facets (commonly 58) are created by grinding and polishing. Popular cuts are round brilliant, oval, marquise, emerald and pear. Odd or old-fashioned cuts make a stone less valuable.

If you are travelling by air, you best bet is to wait and do your liquor and tobacco shopping at Schiphol Airport's tax-free shops. Prices here are competitive and there's a wide choice. The range available on ferries to the U.K., however, is more limited.

Silver is quality-controlled by government inspectors and you'll find some fine work, old and new. **Gold** cannot be called such unless it is at least 14-carat.

Pewter has a long tradition in Holland. The painter Jan Vermeer was perhaps its first publicist in his 17th-century masterpieces. It's decorative as well as useful, and you can buy anything from a Dutch pewter ashtray, for just a few guilders, to an expensive traditional pot-bellied kettle.

Antiques are available in profusion. You'll have a field day – if you've the money to spare. Of Amsterdam's many antique shops, almost a hundred of them are clustered in Nieuwe Spiegelstraat and the nearby streets. It's no coincidence that they are to be found close to the Rijksmuseum: the first of them opened soon after the museum itself, the dealers wanting to emphasize their association with fine art.

You'll pay top prices while benefitting from a great deal of expertise. But remember that many of the items on sale here are said to have come originally from Britain or France.

Traditionalists say clogs are healthy and hard-wearing.

The Tile Standard

Ceramics have been a Dutch passion for centuries but the humble tile has only recently become a collector's item. Now, antique dealers in Amsterdam say that the tile standard has taken over from the gold standard. The rarest ones can cost a small fortune.

Since the first Dutch tiles were made in the 17th century, many people have wanted their kitchens lined with them, for they are clean, durable, and highly attractive. Modern tiles, it's agreed, are a poor substitute. They are thinner, and altogether too exact in design and glaze. Really old tiles are often distinguished by the type of mortar clinging to them, by their thickness, and by the quality of design and glaze. Old bird motif tiles are rare and expensive, for example, and ships with three masts are collector's items, especially if they have a three-coloured flag.

Traditional Dutch tile production stopped over a century ago, but dealers still manage to find them, as often in a lowly farmhouse as in some palatial mansion. Prices are highly variable.

Delft gave its name to an earthenware pottery as early as the 16th century. Now the name makes most people think of a particular kind of blue-and-white tile, and the blue-and-white porcelain originally based on Chinese designs imported in the 17th century.

Both can be found in Amsterdam antique shops, and the porcelain is still produced in Delft today. Beware of imitations, and seek out a well-established store or an obviously expert dealer if you intend to invest a lot of money in it.

Makkum pottery is more delicate in colour and design and preferred by many local people. The genuine article is hand-painted and has the word Makkum on every piece.

101

Markets

Open-air shopping is a way of life. Many Dutch people still go out to buy fresh produce every day: others make a Saturday morning expedition. Both specialist and general markets may open on specific days or every day. Visitors will no doubt hear about the flea-market on Waterlooplein, but here's a selection from the varied range found all over the city.

General markets. The biggest takes up most of **Albert Cuypstraat** just south of the city centre (Monday-Saturday). Others are **Nieuwmarkt** in the old city centre (Monday-Saturday), **Dapperstraat,** near Artis (Tuesday-Saturday), **Noordermarkt,** Jordaan (Monday morning and Saturday) and **Lindengracht,** Jordaan (Saturday).

Specialist markets include: **antiques** at Nieuwmarkt (Sundays, May-October) and indoors at Elandsgracht 109 (Saturday-Thursday); **artists' work** on Thorbeckeplein (spring to autumn on Sundays); **books** at Oudemanhuispoort (Monday-Saturday) and Spui (Fridays); **flowers** at Singel near Munttoren (Monday-Saturday); **pets and birds** at Noordermarkt (Saturdays).

Souvenirs

Little wooden shoes (and Delft versions of the same), miniature windmills and dolls in folk-costume are just about everywhere. For something unusual, try the old Jordaan area of Amsterdam (see p.35).

It has gained a reputation for interesting shopping only **102** in the last few years, and has no defined pattern. But you can find all sorts of off-beat shops along the narrow streets, some in cellars selling old bottles, unusual teas, exotic spices, beads, candles in 5000 different shapes and sizes, rattan and bamboo basketwork, lampshades and crafts of some of the different ethnic groups who have settled here.

Eating Out

Amsterdam claims to offer more variety in cuisine and restaurants than any other city in Europe, including London. This is really an exaggeration, but it's certainly among the leaders.

Traditionally, pride of place has gone to Indonesian cuisine, ahead of the native Dutch in popularity. Owing to the influence of three centuries of colonial presence in the Far East, you are more likely to find Indonesian than traditonal Dutch restaurants – at least in most of The Netherlands' major towns.

RESTAURANTS

(The Berlitz EUROPEAN MENU READER includes an extensive glossary of Dutch (and Indonesian) food with English equivalents in a handy, pocket-sized reference book.)

While Indonesian and Chinese restaurants are the most numerous within Amsterdam's compact city centre, the remarkable international list also takes in Surinamese, Spanish, Thai, Japanese, Greek, Hungarian, French, Italian, Pakistani, Turkish (with belly-dancers) and Kurdish, among others. One or two English and Irish pubs provide their own idiosyncratic food. Several macrobi-

F it for a rajah, the rijsttafel is a succulent and vast experience, adopted by the Dutch.

otic and vegetarian establishments cater to the green-minded, and various steakhouses to the carnivores.

So, can you go Dutch? Strangely, true local cuisine is harder to find. A few places proclaim themselves *Dutch restaurant*, in English, on the door, and some put up a red, white and blue sign shaped like a dish to indicate Dutch home-cooking on the menu.

About 40 restaurants in the city offer a 'tourist menu'. This sign, accompanied by a fork motif, proclaims the availability of a set-price, three-course meal with little or no choice. This is generally good, simple fare, and excellent value for money.

Most menus are printed in two or three languages, almost always including English (though occasionally you will find it is only in French).

All taxes and service charges will be included in your bill, but it's customary to round off payment or give an extra guilder or two if you feel the service has been particularly good.

Amsterdam's restaurants are as varied in atmosphere as in their menus. You can dine with a top-floor view over the city or in a cellar at canal water level, in a windmill or a former church.

So here's to good eating in Amsterdam, or *eet smakelijk*, as the Dutch say.

Eating Indonesian Style

Let's start off with what the Dutch have come to regard as a national speciality of their own, the Indonesian *rijsttafel* (literally, rice-table).

There are up to 32 items in a *rijsttafel*. When this overwhelming array arrives at your table, together with rice and a large soup bowl, tackle the feast this way: put a mound of rice in the centre of your plate, and build around the edges of the mound with spoonfuls from your dishes of *babi ketjap* (pork in soya sauce), *daging bronkos* (roast meat in coconut-milk sauce), *sambal goreng kering* (spicy pimiento and fish paste), or *oblo-oblo* (mixed soya beans).

Anything containing the word *sambal* will be peppery-hot, especially the tiny portions of *sambal* which masquerade as ketchup but will incur a small explosion.

Even the dish of mixed fruit in syrup, *rudjak manis*, will be spicy hot. All in all, what with the crisp, puffy shrimp bread, sour cucumber, cut-up chicken, nuts, fried bananas – not forgetting the skewers of cubed meat with peanut sauce called *sateh* – the rice-table is an unforgettable eating experience.

If you can't tackle the full *rijsttafel*, you might like to try the smaller and cheaper *nasi rames*, commonly called a *mini-rijsttafel*, a single serving on a plate. A *nasi rames* will cost about half the price of a *rijsttafel*, depending on size and restaurant.

Going Dutch

Most non-specialist restaurants offer a mélange of international cooking – entrecôtes, schnitzels, spaghetti dishes etc. – with just a few distinctive Dutch twists. *Biefstuk* for example, is a steak, but always pan-fried, not grilled. Home-fried potatoes, in the Dutch version, are sliced; Dutch chips are deep-fried twice over, golden and crispy.

Holland's famous pea soup *erwtensoep*, (pronounced AIRTE-SOOP) is rich and thick, a small meal in itself, served with smoked sausage and a slice of *pumpernickel*. This, or the other native soup speciality, *bruine bonensoep* (red kidney-bean soup), will often be found on the menu of traditional Dutch restaurants along with the country's variety of winter-warming potato hashes, headed by *hutspot*, a mix of potatoes, carrots and onions, sometimes supplemented with *klapstuk* (beef). *Stamppot* is the generic name for potato and vegetable hashes, which are often hollowed out on top to make room for a fat Dutch sausage *(worst)*. *Boerenkool*, incorporating curly kale, is the most famous *stamppot*.

Fish in Amsterdam is fresh and excellent. Sole *(tong)* is plentiful and served in a dozen **105**

classical French ways: with fruit, shrimp, mushrooms, or wine sauce, or even just poached or grilled on its own. There's also good fresh salmon *(zalm)*, halibut *(heilbot)*, turbot *(tarbot)*, cod *(kabeljauw)*, haddock *(schelvis)* as well as local oysters *(oesters)* and mussels *(mosselen)* – try them steamed, with mustard sauces. Smoked eel *(gerookte paling)* is a rich treat you shouldn't miss; so is Dutch fresh herring and pickle.

If Dutch meat tends to vary widely in quality, local vegetables are always first class. For the main course there's a full range of peas *(erwtjes)*, beans *(bonen)*, spinach *(spinazie)*, carrots *(worteltjes)* and brussels sprouts *(spruitjes)* to choose from. An agreeable Dutch habit from colonial days is to sprinkle some nutmeg on greens.

Salads are good, but limited in style – a routine presentation of lettuce, tomato, green peppers and raw onion liberally doused with an oil and vinegar dressing. They are usually served with the main

Y ou can find friendly local bars and cafés, with friendly locals, all over Amsterdam.

meal. For a salad starter try 'Russian egg' (*russisch ei*), a hard-boiled egg with fish and raw vegetables, or 'Hussars' salad' (*huzarenslaatje*), a creamy mix of potato, raw vegetables and meat.

The Dutch don't have cheese after the main course; they prefer their Edam, Gouda and *Leidsekaas* (Leiden cheese) at lunch and breakfast.

They're not great dessert eaters either, but that's no reason for you to follow suit. Dutch apple tart (*appeltaart*) is usually available, stuffed with apples, sultanas and cinnamon. *Flensjes* are thin pancakes.

Breakfast

With such a hearty meal (*ontbijt*) to start the day, it's no wonder the Dutch still can't tackle a dessert after dinner.

Three of four kinds of bread (including currant bread and a rye bread) are mandatory accompanied by ham, sliced cheese, jam, fruit juice and a boiled egg, as often as not.

Paradoxically, the more expensive your hotel, the less likely that breakfast will be included, whereas the small family hotels will include this formidable feast with the price of the room.

Snacks

Here, the well-known Dutch sandwich shops (*broodjeswinkels*) come into their own. They are fast on service, appear to never close, and always have the price list prominently displayed.

A sandwich (*broodjes*) is likely to be almost a meal in itself – stuffed with maybe five or six slices of ham, cheese or liver sausage, or fillets of herring, or overflowing spoonfuls of shrimp.

Another Dutch tradition is pancakes (*pannekoeken*). On Sunday afternoons in particular, you'll see whole families popping out for pancakes. They're a really substantial snack, offered in a wide range, both savoury and sweet. Try *stroopwafels*, doused with maple syrup, or *poffertjes*, shell-shaped dough balls fried in butter and sugar. Dutch cakes and biscuits are also always filling and tasty.

Drinks

All Dutch restaurants are licensed to serve beer, wine and spirits. All **wine** is imported (there's a wide range of French and German vintages). To economize, ask for a carafe or glass of house wine *(huiswijn)*.

Along with **coffee, beer** (pils) is the national drink, served normally from the tap. It's a deliciously consistent, light-coloured lager, stronger than standard British or American beer, and is cooled to a temperature of 45–46°F (7–8°C). The standard Dutch beer glass holds .22 of a litre, not much more than a third of a pint, and not counting the two fingers of froth on top which local drinkers expect. Many

bars have a range of special and flavoured beers – ask the advice of the barman.

If you would like to learn more about the brewing process, there are tours available, starting at the Heineken building on Stadhouderskade, just east of the Rijksmuseum. from Monday-Friday, 9.30 a.m. and 11 a.m. Tours last almost two hours. There's a small charge to deter those just interested in the free samples.

Dutch **brandy** *(vieux)* is half the price of cognac and milder. *Jenever* is a juniper-flavoured drink along the lines of English **gin** but less strong. It is served chilled in special small glasses, topped almost to overflowing, and should be drunk without tonic, orange juice or any other mixer. There are the clear *jonge* (young) *jenevers*, and the *oude* (old), which are more mature and yellowish in colour. The malt variety is called *Korenwijn* and can compete with the best malt whiskies.

Inquisitive strangers are advised to test the *jonge* to begin with, and you might like to try the special flavoured *je-nevers* such as *bessen* (black-currant) or *citroen* (lemon).

Coffee (*koffie*), the national drink, must be freshly made, or the Dutch will send it back to the kitchen. It's usually served black, but accompanied by a small jug of Dutch *koffiemelk*, a thick, canned, evaporated milk which should be used sparingly if you want to retain the proper taste from the coffee.

Tea (*thee*) is usually served in tea-bag form with lemon, but it is usual for visitors to ask for milk too.

BARS AND CAFÉS

Amsterdam's bars and cafés open at all sorts of hours, but the general pattern is from mid-morning or mid-afternoon until 1 a.m., extending to 2 a.m. on Friday and Saturdays.

Children are allowed in, and you don't have to be a regular to feel at ease in most Dutch bars, though there are a few that cater to special sorts of clientèle. You should be able to detect quickly if you're in one that doesn't suit you.

Most authentic are the city's 'brown cafés' (*bruine cafés*), so called because they are usually dark-wood pan-elled and nicotine-stained. Even the newer ones are likely to be a hundred years old.

You'll find them through-out the old city centre, with some good examples in Spui-straat, Raadhuisstraat, and in the Jordaan district, where idiosyncrasies abound. Here you'll find various bars – old, new and trendy "post" modern cafés. You may see working-class locals singing grand opera on a Sunday afternoon, accompanied by a lone accor-dionist; bars for chess-players, students or fashion models; and bars where a museum curator is quite likely to be rubbing shoulders with a flea-market stallholder.

A variation on the brown café is the *proeflokaal*, or 'tasting house', where there might be a choice of 60 differ-ent beers, countless *jenevers,* and other, even more esoteric intoxicants.

109

Useful expressions for dining out

To help you order ...

Could we have a table?	**Heeft u een tafel voor ons?**
Do you have a set menu?	**Heeft u een vast menu?**
I'd like a/an/some ...	**Ik zou graag ... willen hebben**

beer	**een pils**	napkin	**een servet**
bread	**een brood**	pepper	**de peper**
coffee	**koffie**	potatoes	**aardappelen**
cutlery	**een bestek**	rice	**rijst**
dessert	**dessert**	salad	**sla**
fish	**vis**	salt	**het zout**
glass	**een glas**	soup	**soep**
ice-cream	**ijs**	sugar	**de suiker**
meat	**vlees**	tea	**de thee**
menu	**een menu**	vegetables	**groente(n)**
milk	**melk**	(iced) water	**(ijs) water**
mustard	**mosterd**	wine	**wijn**

...and read the menu

aardbeien	strawberries	**meloen**	melon
ananas	pineapple	**patates frites**	French fries
biefstuk	steak	**perzik**	peach
bloemkool	cauliflower	**pruimen**	plums
citroen	lemon	**rundvlees**	beef
ei(eren)	egg(s)	**sinaasappel**	orange
forel	trout	**uien**	onions
frambozen	raspberries	**uitsmijter**	ham, roast beef
kaas	cheese		or cheese and
karbonade	chop		eggs on bread
kersen	cherries	**varkensvlees**	pork
kip	chicken	**verse paling**	fresh eel
konijn	rabbit	**warme**	
kool	cabbage	**gehaktbal**	meatball
lamsvlees	lamb	**worstje**	sausage

BLUEPRINT for a Perfect Trip

An A-Z Summary of Practical Information and Facts

Listed after most main entries is an appropriate Dutch translation, usually in the singular.

A

ACCOMMODATION (*hotel; logies*)

(See also CAMPING, and HOTELS & RESTAURANTS section on p.65).
The strong guilder makes Amsterdam accommodation seem expensive to travellers from weaker currency countries. Nevertheless, there's a wide range available, from luxury international palaces to small family canalside hotels. Single rooms cost 25-40% less than a double. Service charges and tax are included in room rates, but normal additional tipping of staff is customary.

During holiday periods, when the whole town seems to be brimming with out-of-town visitors, the VVV tourist information office opposite Centraal Station runs admirable booking services, although you may have to stand in a queue to reach the desk. They rarely fail to find a room, though it may well cost more than your intended price range. An alternative is the Netherlands Reservations Centre (NRC), PO Box 404, 2260 AK Leidschendam, Holland. Tel. (070) 320 2500. Fax (070) 320 2611. It is advisable to book in advance at peak times.

Dutch tourist information offices will give you a hotel list which incorporates a one- to five-star assessment based on facilities and prices. Off-season rates are reduced by a small amount. In all but the luxury-class and many first-class hotels, breakfast is usually included in the room rate (but check beforehand). It will normally involve a copious Dutch breakfast (see p.107), not just a light continental starter for the day.

Boarding houses (*pension*), not bookable through the VVV service, are even cheaper than a moderate hotel.

For the motorist there are a few motels around Amsterdam, and most surrounding towns and villages boast at least one hotel, where accommodation will be clean, quiet, friendly, and probably about 30% cheaper than its counterpart in the big city.

Some private houses, especially in villages, offer bed and breakfast at economical prices.

Youth hostels (*jeugdherberg*). The authorities encourage young people not to sleep rough. The addresses and prices of cheap accommodation – including 'official' and unofficial youth hostels – are given in the above-mentioned hotel list. Otherwise, you can call Nederlandse Jeugdherbergcentrale, Prof. Tulpstraat 2, Amsterdam, tel. 551 31 55.

AIRPORT (*luchthaven*)

Schiphol, nine miles (15kms) south west of Amsterdam, is a showpiece modern airport, with moving walkways, conference rooms, good restaurants, snack-bars, a hotel information desk, currency exchange services, a post office, car rental counters, a children's nursery, hair salons, extensive tax-free shops etc. Porters (*kruier*) are scarce, but free baggage trolleys are plentiful.

Every 15 minutes a KLM-hotel bus leaves for the major hotels in Amsterdam. Tickets are sold in the arrival hall. A train leaves every 30 minutes for Amsterdam's Centraal Station, with direct connections to places all over The Netherlands. The journey from the airport takes about 15 minutes and costs about *f*15 single and *f*27.50 return. For flights with KLM or with an airline for which KLM handles the formalities, passengers can check in at the KLM desk at Amsterdam, Rotterdam or The Hague central railway stations. Taxis are always available, metered, and with tips included.

A half-hourly train service runs from Amsterdam RAI (Congress Centre) to Schiphol, a 10-minute ride.

For airport information, tel. 601 9111.

B

BICYCLE and MOPED RENTAL (*fietsverhuur; bromfietsverhuur*)

Though most Amsterdammers own a bicycle, there are many rental agencies, one of them at Centraal Station, others scattered throughout the central areas. Several are listed in the *Yellow Pages*. You must pay a substantial deposit; and ensure that you are given a lock.

The cyclist is so much a part of Dutch life that all modern roads include a cycle path. On these paths there are special traffic signs, showing a cycle symbol. In all cases, the cyclist is regarded as a first-class citizen, and has to be treated with respect by the motorist (see also DRIVING). Unfortunately, veterans of the Amsterdam cycle paths don't always show the same respect for fellow riders. If you aren't used to a bike, be careful – Dutch cyclists don't bother too much with traffic rules. And watch out for the trams. If you rent a moped check carefully on the insurance, and wear a crash helmet.

C

CAMPING (*camping*)

The country as a whole is well stocked with campsites. They are usually clean and have full facilities. It's best to book in advance.

Have you room for   **Heeft u plaats voor een**
a tent/a caravan?   **tent/caravan?**

CAR HIRE (*autoverhuur*)

Most major international agencies are represented in Amsterdam, and more than 40 others are listed in the *Yellow Pages* under *Autoverhuur*. Several major car rental companies have counters at Schiphol Airport.

Conditions of hire are usually strictly applied. You'll need a valid national or international driving licence, held for at least 12 months. The driver must be at least 21 years of age (23 for some firms).

It's advisable to take your passport along to the agency, too. CDW (Collision Damage Waiver) insurance is available at a reasonable price, and is recommended. Remember too that parking in Amsterdam is a big problem.

I'd like to hire a car.	**Ik zou graag een auto willen huren.**
today/tomorrow	**vandaag/morgen**
for one day/week	**voor één dag/één week**
Please include full insurance.	**Met een all-risk verzekering alstublieft.**

CHILDREN'S AMSTERDAM

Many of the things you'll want to do will be enjoyed by children as well. Trips on canalboats (including the pedal-powered variety), the Maritime Museum including going aboard the *Amsterdam*, the Tropenmuseum's children's section, Artis (the zoo, aquarium and planetarium) and the miniature town of Madurodam in The Hague – all of these should be popular and will help to avoid overdosing the young on Old Dutch Masters in the Rijksmuseum.

If your child has wandered away, mobilize the first Dutch person you can find – your hotel receptionist, someone at the department store counter, or a passer-by. You may have to go to the local police station, though its more likely that you'll soon find your child being well looked after by an English-speaking Dutch person.

I've lost my child.	**Ik ben mijn kind kwijt.**

CLIMATE

The weather is as unpredictable as Britain's. Summer days can be either rainy and chilly or gloriously hot and dry – or both. In winter, icy-cold weather rarely prevails for more than a few days at a time. It's more often rainy. Spring and autumn are characterized by cooler, equally unstable weather, though mild – even warm – spells are not uncommon.

	J	F	M	A	M	J	J	A	S	O	N	D
°F	39	39	42	51	57	61	67	65	57	51	42	39
°C	4	4	6	10	14	16	19	18	14	10	6	4

Figures shown are approximate monthly averages.

CLOTHING (*kleding*)

For those on holiday, casual comfort is the keynote during the day-time, although businesspeople dress quite formally. In the evening, at the better restaurants and hotels, men are required to wear a jacket and sometimes a tie. In summer a light sweater or wrap may be need-ed in the evenings. Spring and autumn rarely produce balmy days – let alone evenings – and in winter be prepared to wrap up well, for the wind can be piercing – or exhilarating, depending on how you like to look at it. Take a raincoat, light or heavy according to season, and an umbrella: even during a fine, hot summer, brief showers are possible. Comfortable walking shoes are essential, in all seasons. On the beaches, anything goes. Topless sunbathing is general practice, and some well-marked naturist beaches are to be found all along the North Sea coast.

Will I need a jacket and tie?	**Moet ik een jasje en een das aan?**
Is it all right if I wear this?	**Kan ik dit dragen?**

COMPLAINTS

In this well-ordered and efficient country, not much is likely to cause you any grave dissatisfaction. However, if you are not happy with a service or product, try to resolve the matter with the appropriate person on the spot, whether hotel manager, shopkeeper or super-visor. Be as polite and pleasant as you can: the Dutch take even less kindly than most people to being shouted at. If you cannot obtain satisfaction and wish to pursue your complaint, ask the VVV (see TOURIST INFORMATION OFFICES) for help over problems with hotels and restaurants, the Chamber of Commerce (523 66 00) for trade matters and the police if a crime is involved (see POLICE).

CONVERSION CHARTS

The metric system is universal in The Netherlands.

Distance

Fluid measures

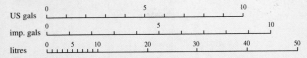

Temperature

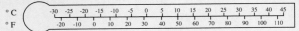

CRIME and THEFT (*misdrijf; diefstal*)

Unfortunately, petty crime and stealing are widespread in Amsterdam. In what was once one of the most innocent of capital cities, even the department stores now display warnings in several languages urging customers to beware of pickpockets. If you do lose your wallet or handbag, report the loss to the nearest police station. Be careful around the red-light district and off the main entertainment squares and avoid carrying a lot of cash or valuable jewellery. It's better to take a taxi home than to walk through the back streets or parks after dark.

Thefts from cars parked in the city have reached hundreds per day (and night). Leave nothing in your car, not even the radio, unless you leave it in a guarded car-park. If it is broken into, or if you have any property stolen, by all means inform the police, but don't expect them to do any more than stamp a report to enable you to make an insurance claim.

I want to report a theft.	**Ik wil aangifte doen van een diefstal.**

117

CUSTOMS and ENTRY FORMALITIES
(*douaneformaliteiten*)

See also DRIVING. The following chart shows what you may take into The Netherlands and, when returning home, into your own country, for your own personal use:

Entering The Netherlands					
From:	Cigarettes	Cigars	Tobacco	Spirits	Wine
1)	200 or	50 or	250 g	1 l. and	2 l.
2)	800 or	200 or	1 kg	10 l. and	90 l.
3)	400 or	100 or	500 g	1 l. and	2 l.
Into:					
Canada	200 and	50 and	900 g	1.1 l. or	1.1 l.
Eire	See 1) and 2) above				
U.K.	See 1) and 2) above				
U.S.A.	200 and	100 and	4)	1 l. or	1 l.

1) EU countries with goods bought tax free, and other European countries
2) EU countries with goods not bought tax free.
3) countries outside Europe
4) a reasonable quantity

Most visitors, including British, American, Canadian and Irish, need only a valid passport – no visa – to enter The Netherlands. (British subjects with U.K. residence can even enter on the simplified Visitor's Passport.) Though European and North American residents are not subject to any health requirements, visitors from certain areas further afield may require vaccinations. Check with your travel agent before departure.

Currency restrictions. From the Dutch side, there are no limits on import or export. But check on your own country's possible restrictions.

I've nothing to declare.   **Ik heb niets aan te geven.**

It's for my personal use.   **Het is voor eigen gebruik.**

DISABLED TRAVELLERS

Many steps have been taken to improve wheelchair access to public buildings, to provide special toilets and in general to take account of special needs. There is still some way to go: Amsterdam's old buildings are not easy to modify. The VVV Tourist Information Office (see p.139) has a leaflet with advice for disabled visitors.

DRIVING

To enter The Netherlands with a car you will require:

- Valid national or international driving licence
- Green Gard – an extension to your regular insurance policy making it valid for travel abroad (Green Card regulations between European countries, especially within the EC, are constantly being relaxed, so check your own insurance when planning your trip).
- Car registration papers
- National identity sticker on back of car
- Red warning triangle for use in case of breakdown

Driving conditions. Drive on the right, pass on the left. Generally, traffic coming from your right has priority. On motorways (expressways), this rule applies only at roundabouts uncontrolled by lights. On other main roads, internationally standardized signs will give you clear right of way over the side roads.

Beware at all times in cities, and especially along the narrow canal-side roads – many local drivers have an ingrained habit of darting out from the right. At every junction along the canals, reduce speed to less than walking pace to avoid the danger of being hit from the right,

Watch like a hawk, in Amsterdam and other cities, for cyclists. At night, many of them ride along almost invisibly, without lights. At all times, remember that you must not cut across them when turning right. Check in your mirror constantly. Be careful also when opening your car door, in case a bicycle runs into it.

Trams have priority over everything on wheels or legs. Watch out and give way to them in any circumstances. Buses leaving from bus stops also have priority.

Motor-cycle, moped and scooter drivers and passengers must wear crash helmets. If a car has seat belts, they must be worn.

Speed limits are well signposted: 20 or 30 mph (30 or 50 kmph) in built up areas, 60 or 75 mph (100 or 120 kmph) on motorways and generally 50 mph (80 kmph) on other roads. Don't waiver from this or you will risk an on-the-spot fine.

Parking. It needs patience, but it can be done. There are very few large public car-parks compared with other cities, for the centre of Amsterdam is densely built-up. Parking is possible along the canal-sides, however, parking tickets bought from automatic ticket dispensers taking *f*2.50, *f*1 and 25c coins, should be displayed in the car clearly visible. Traffic police are vigilant and they don't show any leniency towards cars with foreign plates. Being even a few minutes late could mean a wheelclamp or having your car towed away by traffic police. Either will cost you a lot of money.

Drinking and driving. These two activities are virtually incompatible in The Netherlands. With more than 0.5 millilitres of alcohol in your system per litre of blood (two beers, or the equivalent, at the most) it may be possible for you to lose your driving licence and/or face a hefty fine.

Fuel and oil (*benzine; olie*). Service stations are plentiful and fuel prices fairly standard throughout the country. Fuel is available in 95 octane lead-free (*Euro loodvrij*), 98 octane lead-free (*Super Plus*), 91 octane leaded (*Super*) and diesel. Most stations are self-service. Oil is available in all standard grades.

Breakdowns. Emergency telephones line the motorways at regular intervals. If you're lucky enough to break down just next to a small yellow van bearing a sign *wegenwacht* (WW) on its roof, then the Dutch Automobile Association (ANWB) emergency service is on the spot. The WW's emergency number is 06-0888.

Road signs. International pictographs are in widespread use, but

here are some written signs you may encounter:

Doorgaand verkeer	Through Traffic
Eenrichtingsverkeer	One-way traffic
Einde inhaalverbod	End of no-passing zone
Fietsers	Cyclists
Filevorming	Bottleneck
Gevaarlijke bocht	Dangerous bend
Inhaalverbod	No overtaking (passing)
Let op ...	Watch out for ...
Omleiding	Diversion (Detour)
Parkeerverbod	No Parking
Pas op ...	Attention
Rechts houden	Keep right
Slecht wegdek	Bad road surface
Snelheid verminderen	Reduce speed
Stoplichten op 100 m	Traffic lights at 100 m
Tegenliggers	Oncoming traffic
Uitrit	Exit
Verboden in te rijden	No entry for vehicles ...
Verkeer over één rijbaan	Single-lane traffic
Voetgangers	Pedestrians
Wegomlegging	Diversion
Werk in uitvoering	Roadworks in progress
Wielrijders	Cyclists
Zachte berm	Soft shoulders
(international) driving licence	**(internationaal) rijbewijs**
car registration papers	**kentekenbewijs**
green card	**groene kaart**
Are we on the right road for ...?	**Is dit de goede weg naar ...?**
Fill her up, please, with ...	**Vol, graag, met ...**
super	**super**
regular	**normaal**
Please check the oil/tyres/battery.	**Wilt u de olie/banden/accu controleren?**
I've broken down	**Ik heb autopech**
There's been an accident.	**Er is een ongeluk gebeurd.**

DRUGS

If you've heard that Amsterdam is soft on drugs, beware. The possession of both soft and hard drugs is actually illegal, and there are penalties ranging from four to 12 years for drug offences. Police know well that cannabis/hash is smoked in certain bars and clubs, but their attitude is getting tougher all the time towards dealers in hard *or* soft drugs.

E

ELECTRIC CURRENT (*elektriciteit*)

Everywhere, 220-volt, 50-cycle current is standard. Plugs and sockets are different from both British and American, but your hotel receptionist will usually have an adaptor to spare. American 110-volt equipment will require a transformer.

I'd like a plug adaptor/battery. **Ik wil graag een verloopstekker/een batterij.**

EMBASSIES and CONSULATES (*consulaat*)

Most countries have a consulate in Amsterdam; although the majority of embassies are in The Hague. A complete list can be found in the *Yellow Pages* under *Ambassades/Consulaten*.

Australia: Carnegielaan 10–14, The Hague; tel. (070) 310 82 00.
Canada: Sophialaan 7, The Hague; tel. (070) 361 41 11.
Eire: Dr. Kuyperstraat 9, The Hague; tel. (070) 363 09 93.
New Zealand: Mauritskade 25, The Hague; tel. (070) 346 93 24.
South Africa: Wassenaarseweg 36, The Hague; tel. (070) 392 45 01.
U.K. : Koningslaan 44, Amsterdam; tel. (020) 676 43 43.
U.S.A.: Museumplein 19, Amsterdam; tel. (020) 664 56 61.

Where's the ... consulate? **Waar is het ... consulaat?**
American/Australian/British **Amerikaanse/Australische/Britse**

Canadian/Irish/New Zealand	**Canadese/Ierse/**
	Nieuwzeelandse
South African	**Zuidafrikaanse**

EMERGENCIES (*noodgeval*)

Depending on the nature of the emergency, refer to the separate entries in this section such as EMBASSIES AND CONSULATES, MEDICAL CARE, POLICE, etc. If there's no time, your hotel staff or a taxi driver will certainly help. Language is unlikely to be a problem.

For a real **emergency**, telephone 06-11 (Police, Fire and Ambulance). For the ANWB (Dutch Automobile Association), telephone 06-0888. Here are a few words we hope you will never have to use:

Careful	**Pas op**	Help	**Hulp**
Danger	**Gevaar**	Police	**Politie**
Fire	**Brand**	Stop	**Halt**

ETIQUETTE

Despite the apparent 'anything-goes' attitude, Amsterdammers are quite formal at heart. A handshake on meeting and departure is routine, and a pleasant *dag meneer* ('good-day, sir') or *dag mevrouw* ('good-day, madam') is appreciated as a greeting at almost any time of day. It can be repeated on parting, together with *tot ziens*, a familiar way of saying 'goodbye' or 'see you later'. 'Please' is *alstublieft*, also used in the sense of 'here you are', and 'thank you' is *dank u*.

Although you can expect most of the people you meet in Amsterdam to speak English, it's only polite to ask if they mind if you address them in it before doing so.

GETTING TO AMSTERDAM

Whether you're making a short trip across the North Sea or coming from the other side of the world, the choice of routes and fares to Amsterdam is so varied that the services of a knowledgeable travel agent can be invaluable.

BY AIR

Scheduled Flights. Amsterdam's Schiphol Airport (see also p.113) is one of Europe's busiest and most efficient. It is linked by direct flights to most European and many North American, African and Asian cities. There are also direct flights from Australia, but travellers from New Zealand normally have to fly via Paris or London.

Average journey time between London and Amsterdam is one hour, New York-Amsterdam 7½ hours, Johannesburg-Amsterdam 13 hours, Sydney-Amsterdam 25 hours.

Enquire about reductions on scheduled flights, for example:
- for stays of fixed duration determined in advance
- for passengers under 21
- for students under 26
- for senior citizens (over 60)

A fly-drive arrangement (with hire car at the airport) is particularly attractive if you plan to see the environs of Amsterdam. (If you intend to only stay within the city, however, a car can be more of a liability than a help.)

Charter Flights and Package Tours. Before booking a charter flight or package tour of any kind, be sure to read the date-change and cancellation conditions.

From the British Isles: Package deals including flight (with a choice of several different departure airports), hotel and sometimes excursions as well can mean big savings. At tulip time (April-May) tour operators offer a multitude of arrangements involving various means of transport and different hotel categories.

From North America: ABC (Advance Booking Charter) flights operate from New York, San Francisco and other major U.S. and Canadian cities. Tickets must be bought 30-45 days in advance. OTC (One Stop Inclusive Charter) packages combining air travel with hotel and other ground arrangements at bargain prices are also available. Traditional club charters, cheaper still, have special membership regulations.

From Australia, New Zealand and South Africa: Affinity groups for travellers having shared interests may benefit from special low fares. You may have to be a member for six months before the flight.

BY SEA

Train-Boat-Train. The favourite route from Britain is via Harwich and the Hook of Holland, with departures every day. If you're not much of a sailor, you might prefer the shorter sea route across the Channel to Belgium or France and then a longer train ride north.

Car ferries. Travellers leaving from the south of England will find the Harwich-Hook of Holland or Sheerness-Vlissingen crossings the most convenient. Those visitors coming from the North and Scotland might prefer the Hull-Europoort/Rotterdam service.

Bus-Boat-Bus. Certain British bus companies operate cheap regular services between London's Victoria Coach Station and Amsterdam.

BY RAIL

Visitors from outside Europe who intend to do a lot of rail travel around continental Europe may be interested in purchasing a *Eurailpass*. This flat-rate, unlimited-mileage ticket is valid for first-class travel practically anywhere in western Europe except Great Britain. Visitors under 26 can get the second-class Eurail Youthpass. These tickets must be bought before you leave home.

The *Rail Europ Senior* card, obtainable before departure only, entitles senior citizens (60+) to purchase train tickets for European destinations at reduced prices.

Any family of at least 3 people can buy a *Rail-Europ F* (family) card: the holder pays full price, the rest of the family obtain a 50% reduction in The Netherlands and 14 other European countries; the whole family is also entitled to a 30% reduction in Sealink and Hoverspeed Channel crossings.

Anyone under 26 years of age can purchase an *Interrail* card which allows one month's unlimited second-class travel in some 20 European countries. The Holland Rail Pass, obtainable at any railway station in Holland, entitles the holder to three days' unlimited train travel within a period of 15 days and to discounts on special excursions offered by Netherlands Railways. Up to three children aged between four and 11 years accompanying the holder (who should be over 18) travel for only ƒ3 each.

GUIDES and TOURS

Interpreters (*gids; tolk*). Most city sightseeing and canalboat tours will be accompanied by a multilingual guide. For business or private purposes contact Gidsencentrale, tel. (070) 320 25 45. Interpreters are listed in the *Yellow Pages* under *Tolken*.

Canal Tours (*grachtenrondvaart*). Boats provide interesting tours of the major canals, complete with guide, or at least multilingual tape-recorded commentary on the sights. There are several pick-up points in the city centre (see p.24).

You can choose from all kinds of tours, ranging from the one-hour canal tour to the super 'candlelight tour' with wine and buffet included. You can also hire your own sailingboat (including skipper), a motor boat or a water bicycle.

The Museumboat leaves every 30 minutes between 10 a.m. and 8 p.m. from Centraal Station and stops at Leidsestraat, Rijksmuseum, Leidseplein and Westerkerk.

Many companies operate **bus tours** to sights near and far.

H

HITCH-HIKING (*liften*)

As in most countries, there's less trust on the part of both drivers and hitchers than hitherto, but you'll still see hopefuls trying. It is very much common practice in Holland to hold a card or sign with your destination clearly written on it.

Can you give us a lift to ...?   **Kunt u ons een lift geven naar ...?**

L

LANGUAGE

The Dutch have a talent for languages, and you'll almost never need to feel cut off because of problems with communication. English and German are widely understood and spoken, and French comes a close second. For politeness' sake, don't forget to inquire 'Do you speak English?' before asking a question.

Do you speak English?	**Spreekt u Engels?**
Good morning	**Goedemorgen**
Good afternoon	**Goedemiddag**
Good evening	**Goedenavond**
Please/Thank you	**Alstublieft/Dank u**
You're welcome	**Tot uw dienst**
Goodbye/See you later	**Dag/Tot ziens**

The Berlitz phrase book DUTCH FOR TRAVELLERS covers most situations you're likely to encounter in your travels in Holland and Dutch-speaking Belgium. The Berlitz Dutch-English/English-Dutch pocket dictionary contains a 12,500-word glossary of each language, plus a menu-reader supplement.

LAUNDRY and DRY-CLEANING (*wasserij; stomerij*)
The large hotels offer same-day service (but not on Saturdays, Sundays and holidays). Laundromats (*wasserette*), laundries and dry-cleaners are easy to find, and their prices are considerably lower than those charged by hotels.

When will it be ready?	**Wanneer is het klaar?**
I must have this for tomorrow morning.	**Ik heb dit morgenvroeg nodig.**

LOST AND FOUND PROPERTY (*gevonden voorwerpen*)
For general lost property enquiries, telephone the police on 559 30 05.
Public transport lost property office, tel. 551 49 11.
Taxis lost property, tel. 677 77 77.
Schiphol Airport, tel. 649 14 33. (For property left on the aeroplane itself, telephone the airport police on 601 23 25.)
Trains lost property, tel. 557 85 44.

I've lost my wallet/handbag/passport.	**Ik ben mijn portefeuille/ handtas/paspoort kwijt.**

127

MAPS (*kaarten*)

Road maps of The Netherlands are on sale at petrol stations as well as in bookshops. Very detailed, indexed street plans of Amsterdam and the other main Dutch cities are produced by Falk-Verlag, Hamburg, who also prepared the maps in this guide.

a street map of Amsterdam	**een plattegrond van Amsterdam**
a road map of this region	**een wegenkaart van deze streek**

MEDICAL CARE

See also EMERGENCIES. Medical insurance covering foreign travel is a wise investment. See your travel agent or insurance company about it.

For most residents of the United Kingdom, reciprocal arrangements with The Netherlands ensure that a substantial proportion of emergency medical costs incurred in Holland will be reimbursed. Procedure, which must be strictly observed, is set out in leaflet SA 28 and forms E 111 and CM 1 available from Social Security offices. Travel agents offer supplementary insurance – a worthwhile precaution in view of the high cost of treatment in The Netherlands.

Prescriptions are made up at an *apotheek* (chemist's shop or drugstore). There are always a few on night and weekend duty, the addresses are displayed at every chemist's. You can also telephone 664 21 11 (the same number will advise about emergency doctors or dentists). English and German are widely spoken in medical circles.

a doctor/a dentist	**een arts/een tandarts**
an ambulance	**een ziekenauto**
hospital	**ziekenhuis**
an upset stomach	**maagstoornis**
a fever	**koorts**
Where's the chemist on duty?	**Is er een apotheek in de buurt, die dienst heeft?**

MONEY MATTERS

The unit of Dutch currency is the *gulden*, usually called the guilder, or (more rarely) the florin, in English. It's abbreviated *f, fl, NLG.* or *DFL.*, and is divided into 100 cents (abbreviated *c*). Coins are 5*c* (*stuiver*), 10*c* (*dubbeltje*), and 25*c* (*kwartje*), and 1, 2^1/$_2$, 5 and 10 guilders. Banknotes come in denominations of 10, 25, 50, 100, 250 and 1000 guilders. Prices still incorporate one cent coins, although they no longer exist.

Banks (*bank*). All city banks will exchange foreign money. See also OPENING HOURS.

Currency-exchange offices (*wisselkantoor*). You can change money 24 hours a day at the exchange office of *Grenswisselkantoren* (GWK) in Centraal Station. There are also numerous exchange points throughout the centre which stay open late at night, but beware – they often charge an exorbitant commission.

Credit cards (*credit card*). All major hotels and many restaurants and shops will accept payment by credit card, although some smaller hotels make a surcharge corresponding to the fee they have to pay to the credit card company.

Travellers' cheques (*reischeque*). These are widely accepted, if you have passport identification.

I want to change some pounds/dollars	**Ik wil wat ponden/dollars wisselen**
Do you accept traveller's cheques?	**Accepteert u reischeques?**
Can I pay with this credit card?	**Kan ik met deze credit card betalen?**

NEWSPAPERS and MAGAZINES (*krant; tijdschrift*)

Many major foreign newspapers and magazines, particularly in English and German, are available at shops and news-stands throughout the centre of Amsterdam, at hotels and at Schiphol Airport. London papers will be there from early morning, and for

Americans in particular there's the Paris-based *International Herald Tribune*, with the latest U.S. stock market reports and world news. Have you any English-language newspapers? **Heeft u Engelstalige kranten?**

OPENING HOURS

All banks are open 9 a.m. to 4 p.m. (main branches until 5 p.m.), Monday to Friday (Thursday from 4.30 to 7 p.m.). You can change money seven days a week (24 hours), at the exchange office, Centraal Station.

The Singel 250 post office is open Monday to Friday from 8.30 a.m. to 6 p.m. (Thursday till 8.30 p.m.) and on Saturday mornings from 9 to noon. The Oosterdokskade branch has slightly longer hours: Monday to Friday, 8.30 a.m. to 9 p.m. and Saturday mornings from 9 to noon.

The VVV office at Stationsplein 10 (opposite Centraal Station) is open daily from 8 a.m. to 11 p.m. in July and August. Between September and Easter, hours are 9 a.m. to 6 p.m. Monday to Friday (5 p.m. on Saturday), and from 10 a.m. to 1 p.m. and 2 to 5 p.m. Sundays. From Easter to July, hours are 9 a.m. to 11 p.m. Monday to Saturday, to 9 p.m. Sundays.

Consulates normally open from 9.30 or 10 a.m. to noon and from 2 or 2.30 to 4 or 5 p.m., Monday to Friday.

PHOTOGRAPHY and VIDEO

Developing and printing are of high quality. Numerous one-hour services exist but they are more expensive than normal developing, which will take a couple of days. For black-and-white films, you might have to wait a week.

Using a flash is forbidden in most museums, and in some the camera is banned altogether. Check with the attendant. It may not be quite the same, but good reproductions (transparencies, postcards, prints) are available at all museums.

Video in Amsterdam tends to mean pre-recorded tapes, and they won't be compatible with North American systems. Blank tapes for many kinds of video camera may also be purchased.

I'd like a film for this camera	**Mag ik een film voor dit toestel?**
black-and-white film	**een zwart-wit film**
colour film for slides	**een kleurenfilm voor dia's**
How long will it take to develop	**Hoe lang duurt het ontwikkelen**
(and print) this film?	**(en afdrukken) van deze film?**

PLANNING YOUR BUDGET

To give you an idea of what to expect, here's a list of average prices in Dutch guilders (*f*). They can only be *approximate*, however, as inflation inexorably rises.

Airport transfer. Train Schiphol Airport-Centraal Station *f*5, KLM bus *f*15, taxi f55.

Babysitters. *f*4 per hour up to midnight, *f*5 thereafter, *f*5.50 during daytime.

Bicycle rental. *f*10-15 per day, deposit *f*50-200.

Buses and trams. 3-strip ticket *f*3.50, 10-strip ticket *f*10, 15-strip ticket *f*15. Day ticket for all public transport *f*12.

Camping (per night). *f*10 per person, all in, *f*8 per car, *f*5-8 per tent, children under 9 free.

Canal tours. *f*10-12 for one hour, 'candlelight tour' *f*30-40.

Car hire. Small car: *f*62 per day, *f*0.62 per kilometre; *f*750 per week with unlimited mileage. Medium-size car: *f*88 per day, *f*0.88 per km; *f*1,100 per week with unlimited mileage. Add CDW (collision damage waiver) at *f*25 per day and 18.5% tax. For unlimited mileage daily rates, double the above.

Cigarettes. *f*5 for a packet of 20, *f*8 for a packet of 20 cigarillos, *f*6 for 5 medium-sized cigars.

Guides (personal). *f*170 for half-day, *f*275 for full day.

Hairdressers. Shampoo and set *f*55, permanent wave *f*100, barber's cut *f*20-30.

Hotels. Double room with bath – Luxury *f*350-600, 1st class *f*200-350, medium *f*125-200, moderate *f*85-125 (with shower). Boarding house *f*40-85. B + B *f*18-50. Youth hostel *f*18.50 (members), *f*23.50 (non members).

Meals and drinks. Lunch *f*10-25, dinner *f*25-80, coffee *f*2.50, *jenever f*3-5, gin and tonic *f*10, beer *f*3, soft drink *f*2.50, sandwich *f*3.

Metro. 2 zones *f*2.85. Day ticket for all public transport *f*9.35.

Museums. Normal entry *f*4-12. One-year ticket (passport photo required); up to age 25, *f*15; over age 25, *f*40; senior citizens, *f*25.

To keep costs down, avoid the big hotels and try the many cosy, neighbourhood bars for a drink. Local liquors such as the different *jenevers* will also save you a lot compared to imported ones. If breakfast isn't included in your hotel room rate, you'll find it is cheaper at one of the city's scores of sandwich shops (*broodjeswinkels*) and cafés.

If you're going to sample the nightlife, the discos and small clubs charge no entrance fee but upgrade the drinks in proportion to what is being offered in the way of music, dancing and other attractions. Don't forget a guilder for the cloakroom attendant, and one or two for the doorman, on the way out.

BTW is the abbreviation for Dutch sales tax, the equivalent of British VAT. It's nearly always included in shop and restaurant prices (*inclusief BTW*).

If you make any expensive purchases in The Netherlands, enquire at the point of sale whether tax is included and, if so, whether it could be reclaimed at customs upon your departure from the country. Shops displaying the 'Holland Tax Free' sign, diamond merchants and others accustomed to selling to tourists will be acquainted with the procedures to be followed.

How much is it?	**Hoeveel kost het?**
Have you something cheaper?	**Heeft u iets goedkopers?**
Can we have VAT deducted?	**Kunnen we de BTW aftrekken?**

POLICE (politie)

In Amsterdam you'll see policemen and policewomen patrolling on foot, as well as in small white cars, usually Volkswagens. When trouble occurs, these cars will converge like bees on a hive. City police are dressed soberly in navy blue, with peaked caps, and are courteous to tourists.

The emergency police telephone number (but emergency *only*) is 06-11. For general enquiries, call city headquarters (*hoofdbureau*) at Elandsgracht 117, tel 559 91 11. There are also district stations dotted around town showning a prominent POLITIE sign.

Where's the nearest police station? **Waar is het dichtstbijzijnde politiebureau?**

POST OFFICES (postkantoor)

There are two main post offices and many district offices around town. The head office (*hoofdpostkantoor*) is at Singel 250, at the corner with Raadhuisstraat, just beyond the Royal Palace off Dam Square. The other main office is at Oosterdokskade 3-5 (a little off the beaten track, just east of Centraal Station. See also OPENING HOURS). When buying postcards from stands and souvenir shops, you can usually get the appropriate stamps (*postzegel*) on the spot. Dutch post-boxes are red and have two slots; letters destined for Amsterdam go in the one marked AMSTERDAM, those for other destinations in OVERIGE BESTEMMINGEN.

Mail (*post*)

For longer stays (if you don't know the address beforehand) you can have your mail sent *poste restante* (general delivery) to one of the main post offices mentioned above. Don't forget that identification is necessary when picking up your mail.

Fax. You can send faxes from most hotels, and from the main PTT office, 46-50 Raadhuisstraat, or Tele Talk Center, Leidsestraat 101.

Telegram (*telegram*). The easiest way to send a telegram is to ask your hotel porter or switchboard to send it for you. Otherwise, you can dial the operator (06-0456) who will deal with it. To avoid the chance of an important word being wrongly transmitted, go yourself **133**

to the head post office at Singel 250 for a 24-hour service. (Note if you send one to the UK it will merely be delivered with the mail.)

PUBLIC HOLIDAYS (*openbare feestdag*)

Although banks, offices and major shops close on the eight public holidays, most museums will still be open from 1 to 5 p.m., and it's business as usual in the restaurants and tourist-oriented domains.

January 1	*Nieuwjaar*	New Year's Day
April 30	*Koninginnedag*	Queen's Birthday
December 25 and 26	*Kerstfeest*	Christmas Day and Boxing Day
Movable dates:	*Goede Vrijdag*	Good Friday
	Tweede Paasdag	Easter Monday
	Hemelvaartsdag	Ascension Thursday
	Tweede Pinksterdag	Whit Monday

PUBLIC TRANSPORT

An extensive network of buses (*bus*), trams (*tram*) and underground/subway (*metro*) lines comes to life around 6 a.m. and continues until shortly after midnight. Thereafter nightbuses (*nachtbus*) serve a number of key routes, usually at half-hourly intervals.

For the purposes of local and regional bus, tram and subway travel, the country is divided into some 2000 zones, of which Amsterdam forms six. Fares are therefore calculated in zones corresponding with strips on the *Nationale strippenkaart*, valid throughout the country. Tickets are obtainable from: the tram or bus driver (one-hour tickets, one-day tickets, 3- and 10-strip tickets); at metro stations (automatic ticket dispensers for day tickets and for single trips of one, two, three or four zones); at post offices, at railway stations and at many tobacconists (for 15-strip tickets). Tickets include transfer to other bus, tram or metro lines. *Strippenkaarten* bought in a tram or bus are more expensive than bought elsewhere. There's a heavy fine if you're caught travelling without a ticket.

Stamp your ticket in the yellow stamping machine (for trams, at the rear; for buses, left of the front door; for the metro, near to the stairs leading to the platforms); and *always* use one strip more than the number of zones you are crossing.

If you are planning to spend a day in Amsterdam, buy a day ticket (*dagkaart*), valid for one day and the next night, entitling you to unlimited rides on any of the city's public transport systems. Two-day or three-day tickets are also available at even bigger savings, but they can only be obtained at the GVB ticket booth (*kaartverkoop*) in front of Centraal Station and at the GVB head office at Prins Hendrikkade 108 (near Centraal Station).

For further information, tel 06-9292.

Trains (*trein*). Dutch trains run on time. It's a matter of national pride. Services are frequent and excellent. From Amsterdam you can be in Haarlem in 14 minutes and The Hague in 45. Other destinations are equally well provided for.

Ask about special one-day, seven-day and Holland Rail (three days unlimited travel out of ten) ticket offers. You cannot make seat reservations on domestic trains.

The information bureau at Centraal Station is open daily (see also OPENING HOURS). Take one of the tickets there that assures you your rightful place in the 'queue'. Alternatively, telephone 06-9292 (information about all public transport including international trains).

R

RADIO and TV (*radio; televisie*)

BBC Radio 4 long wave is easily picked up in The Netherlands. For music-lovers, excellent programmes are broadcast from the local Hilversum stations.

All British and American films and series are shown on TV in their original language with Dutch subtitles. Amsterdam has cable television, which enables satellite channels and programmes from neighbouring countries (Belgium, Germany, Britain and France) and CNN to be seen in many hotel rooms.

RELIGION

The formerly strict adherence to one or another Protestant sect or to the Catholic church has declined in recent decades. Many Protestant churches have been deconsecrated and Dutch Catholics have been prominent among those pressing for liberal reform.

In Amsterdam, services (*kerkdienst*) are held on Sundays in English in the following churches:

Catholic: Catholic church in the Begijnhof (at 12.15 pm)

Protestant: English Reformed Church in the Begijnhof (at 10.30 am)
Christ Church (Church of England), Groenburgwal 42 (at 10.30 am and 7.30 pm)
Christian Centre Fellowship, Euromotel, Oude Haagse Weg
Jewish services are held in the synagogues at Jacob Obrechtsplein and Lekstraat 61. In summer, it's possible to attend services at the famous 17th-century Portuguese synagogue near Waterlooplein (tel. 624 53 51/625 62 22).

RESTAURANTS

(see HOTELS and RESTAURANTS section, pp.65-80)

S

SMOKING

The Dutch have recently been cutting down on their formerly prodigious consumption of tobacco, probably as a result of campaigns against smoking.

Cigarettes are usually sold in packets of 25. A full range of both local and international makes are available at tobacconists' *(sigarenhandelaar)* and from vending machines. Hotels and restaurants also sell them. A lot of Dutch people roll their own cigarettes *(shag)*.

The world-famous Dutch cigars, which are not expensive, range from mini cigarillos through medium-sized (and sometimes handmade) varieties to torpedoes of Churchillian proportions. Renowned 136 for their aroma, they use pure Indonesian, particularly Sumatran, tobacco with no additives – a legacy from the colonial days when Amsterdam was the world's biggest tobacco market. Pipe tobacco, from the many famous Dutch manufacturers, is also plentiful.

A packet of cigarettes/A box of matches, please.	**Een pakje sigaretten/Een doosje lucifers, alstublieft.**
Cigars	**Sigaren**
Tobacco	**Tabak**

T

TAXIS (taxi)

They are recognised by a taxi sign on the roof. Generally they do not cruise the streets looking for fares, but return after a job to one of their ranks. If you do spot one with the roof sign lit, it means the cab is free, and you can hail it. You can phone for a taxi, either by calling the radio-controlled *taxicentrale* (677 77 77) or your nearest rank. A novelty is the 'Treintaxi', which operates in 30 towns and takes passengers from the railway station to any place within the municipal boundaries or vice-versa for only f5.

Many places of interest in Amsterdam can also be reached by **water taxi** (622 21 81). Boats take up to eight passengers, plus luggage and bicycles. Fares are shared.

What's the fare to ...?　　　　**Hoeveel kost het naar ...?**

TELEPHONE (telefoon)

You can dial direct from Amsterdam to all of western and most of eastern Europe, and to most of the rest of the world, including the U.S.A., Canada, Australia, New Zealand and South Africa. Most hotels offer direct dial service from rooms. To make an international call, dial 00, wait for the tone, then dial the required country code and area code (omitting the initial 0).

At Telehouse, Raadhuisstraat 46-50, behind Dam Square, there's a 24-hour service for international calls. You can also send fax and telex messages from there.

For some services, you'll have to go through the operator (dial 06-0410). To make a personal (person to person) call, if you want to air your Dutch specify *ik wil een gesprek met voorbericht;* for a reverse-charge (collect) call, say *ik wil telefoneren op kosten van de ontvanger.*

international directory enquiries	06-0418
for international calls through the operator and domestic call information	06-0410

In pay phones you need to insert a 25c coin to call the operator: it will be returned. In card phones insert a card: it will not be charged. Pay phones (coin boxes) accept 25c and f1, f2½ and f5 coins.

TIME DIFFERENCES

The following chart shows the time differences between The Netherlands and various cities in winter. In summer, clocks are put forward one hour in line with neighbouring countries of the EC.

New York	London	**Amsterdam**	Jo'burg	Sydney	Auckland
6 a.m.	11 a.m.	**noon**	1 p.m.	10 p.m.	midnight

TIPPING

Service is always included in hotel and restaurant bills. It is however customary to round up taxi fares and leave a few coins for the waiter in restaurants. The habit has grown of leaving credit card vouchers open for a tip to be written in. If you feel the service has been exceptional, you may like to do so. Some further suggestions:

Hotel porter, per bag	f2	Theatre usher	50 c-f1
Maid, per week	f15	Hairdresser/Barber	included
Lavatory attendant	50 c	Tour guide	5-10%

TOILETS (*toiletten*)

There's a lack of public lavatories in Amsterdam, but the hundreds of café-bars are designated as public places and you may use their toilet facilities. It would seem polite to have a beer or a coffee on the way out.

Most department stores have smart, clean, public toilets, usually with an attendant on duty. Be sure to put a coin or two – at least 35 cents – in the waiting saucer, or you may learn a few new Dutch expressions.

Where are the toilets?   **Waar zijn de toiletten?**

TOURIST INFORMATION OFFICES

Netherlands Board of Tourism (*National Bureau voor Toerisme*) offices, at the addresses given below, will help you when planning your trip.

Australia: 6th floor, 5 Elizabeth St., Sydney, NSW 2000; tel 02-276-921.

British Isles: PO Box 523, London SW1E 6NT; tel (0891) 200277

Canada: Suite 710, 25 Adelaide St. East,, Toronto, Ont. M5C 1Y2; tel (416) 363-1577.

U.S.A.:   355 Lexington Ave., New York, NY 10017; tel (212) 370-7367.
255 N. Michigan Ave., Suite 326, Chicago, IL 60601; tel (312) 819-0300.
90 New Montgomery Street, Suite 305, San Francisco, CA 94105; tel (415) 543-6772.

In individual Dutch towns, tourist affairs are handled by an office of a separate organisation known universally by its abbreviation – VVV (pronounced vay-vay-vay). Blue signs bearing the triple-V guide you to the tourist office from the edge of any town.

Amsterdam's VVV offices are at:

Stationsplein 10, opposite Centraal Station, tel. 06-340 340 66. (Open for long hours which vary with the season.)

Leidsestraat 106, open from 9 a.m. to 5 p.m. except in winter, when they open afternoons only. (See also OPENING HOURS.)

Where is the tourist office?   **Waar is het VVV-kantoor?**

Holland Leisure Card. A card entitling non-residents to substantial discounts on car hire, public transport, domestic air travel, and admission to many tourist attractions, as well as discounts on purchases, **139**

and free entry to casinos. It is valid for one year. It can be purchased at NBT offices (see Tourist Information Offices), selected VVV tourist offices, Dutch Railways (NS) travel agencies and Grenswisselkantoren (at railway stations and border crossings).

VACCINATIONS
No vaccinations are required.

WATER (*water*)
You need have no worries at all, it's perfectly safe (though the native Amsterdammer swears it's not as good as it used to be). When you ask for water in a restaurant, waiters will assume you mean bottled mineral water unless you specify otherwise.

A glass of water, please. **Een glaasje water, alstublieft.**

YOUTH HOSTELS
(See also Accommodation). The VVV tourist information offices have lists of low-price accommodation which include hostels (see also p.113).

USEFUL EXPRESSIONS

(See cover flap for more useful expressions)

yesterday/today/tomorrow	**gisteren/vandaag/morgen**
day/week/month/year	**dag/week/maand/jaar**
left/right	**links/rechts**
large/small	**groot/klein**
old/new	**oud/nieuw**
up/down	**boven/beneden**
hot/cold	**warm/koud**
What does this mean?	**Wat betekent dit?**

NUMBERS

0	**nul**	15	**vijftien**
1	**een**	16	**zestien**
2	**twee**	17	**zeventien**
3	**drie**	18	**achttien**
4	**vier**	19	**negentien**
5	**vijf**	20	**twintig**
6	**zes**	21	**eenentwintig**
7	**zeven**	30	**dertig**
8	**acht**	40	**veertig**
9	**negen**	50	**vijftig**
10	**tien**	60	**zestig**
11	**elf**	70	**zeventig**
12	**twaalf**	80	**tachtig**
13	**dertien**	90	**negentig**
14	**veertien**	100	**honderd**

DAYS

Sunday	**zondag**	Thursday	**donderdag**
Monday	**maandag**	Friday	**vrijdag**
Tuesday	**dinsdag**	Saturday	**zaterdag**
Wednesday	**woensdag**		

Index

143

144